"An amazing memoir ... the story of an American girl and American history—from desert and mountain country to Manhattan, from bare-bones poverty to flourishing old money wealth, from life-broken failures to international celebrities. Gleah Powers's story is moving, but never sentimental, absolutely and fearlessly candid, stocked with surprises and some real shocks. Abused, used for her looks, she never stops to feel self-pity, never stops her search for something transcendent."
JAMES ROBISON, WHITING GRANT WINNING AUTHOR OF NOVELS AND SHORT STORIES

"*Million Dollar Red* takes us on a glorious, whirlwind tour of the author's wild life and dazzling mind. We see her on her picaresque adventures, hanging out with Antonioni in Death Valley, and being ineluctably drawn to the seductive allure of cults. More importantly, we see the narrator figuring out how to be alive. The precision of language and of memory will make you weep, and Powers' dry wit cuts through any risk of sentimentality. This book is an indelible portrait of the US in the '60s and '70s in all its gorgeous, shadowy excess, and a testament to the heart-rending talent of Gleah Powers."
ALISTAIR McCARTNEY, AUTHOR OF *THE DISINTEGRATIONS*

"Divorcées, gamblers, celebrities, cultists? We now live in the culture that Gleah Powers so prophetically explored as a young woman in the 1960s, '70s and '80s ..."
F.X. FEENEY, CRITIC LA REVIEW OF BOOKS, AUTHOR OF *ORSON WELLES: POWER, HEART & SOUL*

"A compelling, fascinating memoir of a woman, who, like her mother before her, tries to find herself through the eyes of men, but who, unlike her mother, is able to step into her own vision and voice. Gleah Powers captures her life with great verve and wit."
GAYLE BRANDEIS, AUTHOR OF *THE ART OF MISDIAGNOSIS: SURVIVING MY MOTHER'S SUICIDE*

"Gleah Powers scales the fortress, braves the unknown, and shares the adventure. She sets a heroic example of how to save your own life, one story at a time."
JILLIAN LAUREN, NEW YORK TIMES BESTSELLING AUTHOR OF *SOME GIRLS: MY LIFE IN A HAREM* AND *EVERYTHING YOU EVER WANTED*

# About the Author

Prior to the publication of her acclaimed first novel *Edna & Luna* in 2016, Gleah Powers led a life by turns grounded and nomadic. Her Phoenix-based grandmother provided a first intermittent refuge against her mother's frequent marriages. By eighteen, Gleah was fully on her own, traveling with the production of Michelangelo Antonioni's *Zabriskie Point*, teaching the great filmmaker—and great insomniac—the card game Gin Rummy while the rest of the crew slept. Thereafter she studied art in Mexico City and Los Angeles, modeled in New York, tended bar, explored the world—and worlds—of adventure which she makes unforgettable in *Million Dollar Red*.

Visit her website: *www.gleahpowers.com*

# Million Dollar Red

## GLEAH POWERS

**Vine Leaves Press**
Melbourne, Vic, Australia

**Million Dollar Red**
Copyright © 2019 Gleah Powers
All rights reserved.

Print Edition
ISBN: 978-1-925965-20-9
Published by Vine Leaves Press 2019
Melbourne, Victoria, Australia

Cover design by Jessica Bell
Interior design by Amie McCracken

A catalogue record for this book is available from the National Library of Australia

# Table of Contents

*…My mother taught me to enunciate, not to eat with my mouth full. Everything else I did myself.*
  ~Carol Potter, "Enunciation," *Some Slow Bees*


*A fatherless girl thinks all things possible and nothing safe.*
~Mary Gordon, *The Company of Women*

Up until the age of thirty, my name was Linda.

# Lucky Streak

After their weekend honeymoon in Las Vegas, my mother and Jack came to pick us up from Long Scraggy Mountain Ranch Camp for Girls in Buffalo Creek, Colorado. My sister, Kimberly, and I had spent a month there swimming in Buffalo Creek. We weaved strips of colored plastic together to make key chains and bracelets, drew pictures of horses, and rode Duke and Pepper through forests of shimmering silver dollar Eucalyptus trees.

We said goodbye to our counselors, walked out of our log cabin, and saw my mother leaning against a new white Lincoln Continental, her arms folded loosely over her flat stomach, thin legs crossed at her ankles. She was the founder of the Arizona Model's Guild, and I knew she'd spent at least two hours putting together the perfect look for today's event. She wore cherry-colored shorts with a matching sleeveless blouse. The jewels on her leather thongs matched the bright red polish on her toenails. Her short, dark brown hair didn't move in the wind. She waved to us like a politician.

"Mommy, Mommy," we cried as we ran through swirling dust toward her tanned legs.

She took off her large tortoise shell sunglasses and bent

down to greet us, careful not to muss her clothes. "Girls, did you have a good time? I missed you so much. How do you like the car?"

Her blue eyes got bigger and rounder. She smiled, hugged us in a thin way, her long angular fingers curled partially around my shoulder. Kimberly grabbed my mother's legs from behind. I moved closer too, put my arms around her hips, smelled her perfume in the fabric of her linen shorts, felt her familiar hipbones against my chest.

"Oh, you're so dusty," she said. She pushed my bangs to the side with her fingernails. "You both need haircuts."

I looked behind my mother and saw the window of the Lincoln slide halfway down. Sunlight bounced off the silver door handle. I stepped back. I saw part of a man's head. Dark green sunglasses hid his eyes. "Who's that?"

My mother stood up straight and smoothed the wrinkles from her shorts.

"Oh, girls," she said as if she'd just remembered something. "I have a surprise for you." Her voice went up an octave. "This is Jack. Jack Lange. We just got married. Do you know what that means? It means you can call him Daddy because that's what he is now. He's your daddy."

My body went stiff. I wanted to scream, *Not this again.* Had he been in our house? In our swimming pool? He better not have been in my room, sat on my new bedspread or touched my ballerina music box. And my mother better keep her promise that when we came home from camp I could take a watercolor class. I was good at the piano and ballet too. But I liked making art the best.

The car window slid all the way down. "Hiya, girls. Have a good time at camp?" He winked at me and took a drag on his cigarette. His teeth had a big space in front.

His hair was short, black, and stuck straight up. This guy didn't look anything like my real father or my mother's second husband, Ed, or any of the men she'd been dating, who were all handsome. "Dreamy," as she said. I couldn't imagine Jack being part of anyone's dream.

"I'm not calling him Daddy."

"Now, Linda." She smiled at him. "It takes her a while to get used to things. You say hello, Kimberly."

"Hi," she said with her finger in her mouth.

"Come on, girls." My mother put her arm around my sister.

"I'm not going anywhere with him," I said.

He got out of the car and opened the back door, bowing from the waist like a chauffeur. Powdery earth streaked across the tops of his shiny black shoes, like rock strata. His body was square-shaped, like a box, but his movements were smooth like a ballroom dancer. Maybe that was the attraction. My mother loved to dance.

"Get in that car, young lady." My mother planted her body behind me and pressed me toward the Lincoln.

I sat behind him, gripping the armrest on the door. He took off fast. Dust clouds enveloped us. I couldn't see out the window. If I hadn't been at camp, I was sure I could have stopped this.

My mother turned to us with wide eyes and all her teeth showing. In her cheeriest voice, she asked, "So, how were the counselors?"

This was our cue to imitate her—the eyes, and the smile—for his benefit, continuing to pretend we were thrilled with her surprise. It didn't matter that I wouldn't play along.

I put my arm around Kimberly and pulled her across

the backseat close to me. "Don't worry," I whispered. "I'll think of something."

"Okay," she said, looking puzzled. She was only eight, two years younger than me.

I looked through the back window. The dust had cleared. There was nothing but empty highway in both directions. Jack smoked cigarettes and drove ninety miles an hour. When he passed a slower car, we almost rammed into an oncoming truck. "That was close," he said laughing. My mother and sister didn't seem scared. I gripped the armrest harder.

"My cabin counselor was named Judy," said Kimberly. "She was neat."

"Did you have enough underwear?" my mother asked. She pulled down the mirrored visor and checked her make-up, putting one red fingernail in the corner of her eye and flicking out the eyeliner that had collected there. "I hope you didn't lose any after all those nametags my dressmaker sewed in."

"We got to sleep outside by a fire," Kimberly said with a big grin.

"That sounds like fun," said Jack. "Did you tell scary stories?"

I rolled my eyes and looked away. I'd been through this "winning over the children" bit before.

"Real scary," said Kimberly. "One about cowboy ghosts who might sneak up on you in the night and brand you on the bottom like a cow."

*Oh, boy*, I thought. *What a fool to tell this guy anything.* I pulled my legs up onto the car seat.

"Well girls," Jack said. "Your mother and I have planned a little trip to the fishing lodge in Oak Creek Canyon. What do you think of that?"

"Goody," said Kimberly. "Do we get to go to Slide Rock?"

"We'll do it all," said my mother. "We're a real family now." She dangled her charm bracelet in front of us pointing to the new gold, heart-shaped charm inscribed with *I married 3 angels*. Bigger than all the other charms. His hung between my baby ring and my mother's sorority pin.

What a phony. This guy was worse than I thought. He kept looking at me in the rear view mirror. I pictured poison arrows stuck in the back of his neck. I'd won three archery medals at camp. I moved closer to the armrest so he couldn't see me, wishing the door would open and I would fall out, splatter on the highway. Maybe then she'd stop smiling. I didn't care how new the car was. He was a big mistake.

My mother divorced my real father when I was three. She and her second husband, Ed, were only together for two years. Later, she said she only married him because she thought he would make a good father. She neglected to find out whether or not we liked him, which we didn't. I overheard her tell her friends she divorced him because he didn't want to have sex. "I think he wanted to be a priest," she said.

Now she was ruining everything again.

"I'll bet you girls are hungry," said Jack as he pulled into the Howard Johnson's parking lot. "Your mother's told me how much you like pancakes."

Inside the diner, my shoes touched his knees as I slid into a sticky orange booth across from him. I snatched my legs up under me, glad that I'd probably left dirt on his black pants.

They ordered coffee from the waitress.

"So," he said to me, "Ever been fishing?"

He lit a cigarette. I noticed his watch was too tight. I didn't answer.

"How about you, Kimberly?"

"I like it."

"You've never been fishing," I said.

"I still like it." She slapped her tiny hand on the table.

I could tell Jack was touching my mother under the table. Her head tilted up at him. His shoulder moved as he rubbed his hand up and down, probably making red marks on her thigh.

"When we get home, I thought I'd buy you girls a horse," said Jack.

"It's not your home," I said under my breath.

"Oh, boy," said Kimberly. "I know how to ride English and Western. Linda only knows Western."

"Yeah. But I won ribbons for barrel racing."

The waitress, whose nametag said Faye, came back to the table. She said, "Hey, cutie. It can't be all that bad." She smacked her gum and said, "Maybe breakfast will cheer you up. Whatdaya say, honey?"

Faye had red, curly hair and dark blue eye shadow with gold flecks on her eyelids. She wore fruit earrings, tiny cherries and bananas. My mother hated pierced ears. She said it was cheap looking and so was chewing gum. I liked Faye. I wanted her to tell me what to do about our mother.

I ordered blueberry pancakes.

Faye said, "That should make you feel better, honey." She took my menu.

Jack and my mother ordered sausage and eggs, sunny side up. He winked at Faye and smiled as he handed over their menus.

When Faye left the table, my mother turned to him.

"That waitress looks so much older than I do." She pushed her hair back with red fingernails. "And I'll bet we're the same age."

"You're beautiful, Gail," Jack said and squeezed her hand.

After breakfast, at the cash register, Jack offered to buy us a box of salt-water taffy.

"Yeah," said Kimberly, with her buckteeth showing. "I want the biggest box."

"Forget it," I said.

When he turned his back to pay the check, my mother grabbed my arm and looked at me with a tight mouth. "I've had about enough of this," she said, her eyes flashing. "You're acting very spoiled. He's the best thing that's happened to us. He's very bright and he'll make a wonderful father."

Three of my mother's favorite expressions were "spoiled rotten," "self-centered" and "very bright." Very bright usually didn't go with self-centered or spoiled rotten. Everyone she talked about fell into one or more of these categories unless they were too boring to mention.

"I don't like him," I said.

"Of course you do."

Jack turned towards us. She smiled at him and let go of my arm.

Back in the car, he turned on the radio. Johnny Mathis was singing "Chances Are." Jack sang along and looked at my mother. They were touching each other again in the front seat. I wanted to throw up my pancakes.

As we drove through cow pastures, we saw a bull up on one of the cow's backs. Under his breath, I heard Jack say, "Cow fucking" to my mother.

"What's that?" Kimberly asked me in a whisper.

"I'll tell you later." I'd learned the word at camp. I couldn't imagine my mother doing that with him. They laughed, turned up the radio, and talked in low voices.

Jack drove all day through the dry, quiet desert. We passed tabletop mesas and red buttes full of uneven holes. Stone columns stood alone, their layers stacked like blocks. We stopped at the Four Corners monument. Jack said it was the only place in the country where four states came together in one place. He got out and put each of his hands and feet in the states of Arizona, New Mexico, Utah and Colorado at the same time. Kimberly tried it too but she wasn't tall enough. *How stupid*, I thought. Didn't he know there weren't any real borders in the desert?

We drove two more hours on Route 66 to Gallup, New Mexico and spent the night at the Tewa Lodge. The six rooms were built like teepees, wrapped in thick canvas, and painted white with Zuni Indian designs on the sides. The front doors faced a circular courtyard with a small swimming pool. My mother and Jack were in one teepee. Kimberly and I had our own. The inside walls were painted turquoise. The windows were diamond-shaped cutouts. Small rocks had been glued around the outside edges to hide someone's uneven cutting job. I could see my mother in her teepee across the pool, but I wanted her to spend the night with us, not over there.

Kimberly propped up her pillows and stretched out on one of the beds. "What does that fuck word mean?"

"Never mind. What are we going to do?" I sat on the other bed.

"He bought taffy," said Kimberly.

"So what?"

"And we get a horse."

"You're so easily fooled. Like you were with Ed."

"Well, I like this guy."

She was too young to remember that Ed had tried to act like a father too. When he got a new advertising job in Texas, we had to move to Fort Worth where the trees in our front yard were so skinny they had to be held up with sticks. Ed bought us a playhouse for the backyard and joined the Ridgley Hills Country Club so Kimberly and I could take swimming lessons and meet the right people. I had a hard time making friends, but my mother said the girls there were too fat to be friends with anyway.

I had flying dreams. Ed and other people I didn't know chased me down the street. Just before they caught me, when I had no more breath, I would lift up with great relief and fly away over the Ridgley Hills rooftops toward the stars. I began to practice flying after school. Wearing special red tennis shoes, I tried to recreate how my body felt in the dreams. Kimberly would fan me, bring Cokes and measure the distance each time I jumped out into the backyard from the three-foot-high patio. My first goal was to fly to the corner of the fence.

Kimberly would call out instructions. "Not enough lift. Run faster before you jump."

Now in the teepee, Kimberly turned onto her side. "Remember when it snowed in Fort Worth? And the summer that giant tarantula climbed up our street? It was as big as the moon and nobody knew where it came from. I wanted to keep it for a pet, but Mommy wouldn't let me. I know Ed was in the house, but I don't remember ever talking to him. He had that dog food last name. Did we ever call him Daddy? What happened to him anyway?"

"I don't know. Maybe he didn't like us enough."

"This guy is better."

"I wonder how long he'll stay."

Kimberly turned away and went to sleep in her clothes. My mother's dim laugh floated across the water. I wished Kimberly could see that Jack wasn't any different from Ed. I'd have to come up with a plan.

I considered running away. At midnight, I got a Coke and some peanut butter crackers at the vending machine. I walked to the highway but there was nothing, not even a truck, only the black desert under a sky of ancient blinking stars. Back in the room, I stayed awake, lying like a board under the dark brown bedspread, a puffy yellow arrow pattern in its center, longing for a flying dream.

\*\*\*

When the sun rose the next morning, the teepees across the courtyard turned stark white while others, including ours, became pale gray shadows. I got up and went to the sunny side of the pool. The smell of chlorine wafted through the dry air. I sat on a lounge chair, closed my eyes and said a prayer asking God to get rid of this guy. It was the only thing I could think of.

Pretty soon, I heard a flapping sound. It got closer and closer. I opened my eyes and there was Jack in a bathing suit that stretched around his square-shaped body. A blue-striped hotel towel blocked me from picturing more poison arrows stuck in his neck.

"Going swimming? Your mother tells me you're quite a swimmer."

"I guess."

He slid off his flip-flops and dove into the deep end. It was my chance to run, but I didn't. I kept watching him. I wanted to learn to dive.

His head popped up, and he swam to the edge of the pool, near where I was sitting. His mouth was full of water. He squirted it in a long thick stream through the space in his front teeth. It almost touched my feet.

"How'd you do that?" I said, pulling my legs up.

He took another gulp, squirted again, and that time the water did touch my feet.

"Come on in and I'll show you."

"I don't think so." I got up and walked away.

"See ya at breakfast then."

***

At the fishing lodge in Oak Creek Canyon, I sat alone at the edge of the stream in front of our cabin while Jack and Kimberly stood in the water in black boots and floppy hats. A curved wicker basket hung over his shoulder to hold the fish they caught. He put bait on their fishing pole hooks and showed her how to throw out her line.

My mother set up a lounge chair, angling it between the trees for sunbathing. "The sun is the only thing that relaxes me," she said. She rubbed baby oil on her legs and stretched out in her sleek black bikini, flipping the pages of *Vogue* magazine probably looking for the latest Oleg Cassini designs for her dressmaker to copy. *Vogue* gave my mother all kinds of advice—to stay slim, eat standing up to burn more calories, and have only one slice of bread on a sandwich. Open-faced they called it. But sometimes I saw her eat a whole bag of ginger snaps for lunch.

The creek made a soft clapping sound as it rolled in front of me. I moved closer to the edge, leaned over and saw my face in the water shimmering in pieces, like a jigsaw puzzle. Every now and then, Jack glanced over and waved at me.

Kimberly's pole jerked up and down. Her voice cracked across the canyon, "I got a fish." It slithered and gagged on the hook, helpless. It squirmed and slapped around in Jack's hands as he tried to unhook it and slide it into the wicker basket. I couldn't watch. I ran into the woods, imagined myself getting lost and never found.

My mother called out, "Don't you want to get some sun, Linda?"

*** 

In the lodge dining room, red and gray Navajo rugs hung on either side of a river-rock fireplace. On each table, baskets woven with black triangular designs held thick pieces of dark crusted bread wrapped in cloth napkins.

"Where's the menu?" I said.

"There is no menu," my mother said. "They only serve fish." She was slightly freckled from her day in the sun.

"I want steak."

My mother frowned. "You have no choice. Now, put your napkin in your lap. You too, Kimberly."

"I can't eat fish," I said to Jack. "One time I almost choked to death on the bones."

"No, you didn't," my mother said.

"I did. You weren't there. It was at Corrine's house."

"Don't worry about bones," Jack said. "I'll take care of that."

The dead trout came to the table on a big white platter. Their eyes looked alive, and their rainbow colors had been cooked out of their bodies.

Jack picked up a long shiny knife. "Watch this."

I held my hand over my eyes and peeked out through cracked fingers. He slit each fish open, one by one, and magically pulled out the whole skeleton with every bone attached.

I dropped my hand and said, "How'd you do that?"

"Wow!" said Kimberly.

"He knows how to do lots of neat things, don't you, Jack?" my mother said. "He's like Superman."

He winked at me.

I pushed pieces of trout toward the edge of my plate in a lopsided star pattern so it looked like I'd eaten some. I couldn't stop staring at the skeleton fish. Their eyes stared at me from the platter.

\*\*\*

Back at our house on Third Avenue, a row of dark pants hung upside down from wooden hangers in my mother's closet. A stuffed quail sat displayed on an unfamiliar table in the den. His opera records filled our record cabinet. A silver electric razor, a push-up container of Old Spice deodorant, and a bottle of men's cologne lined one side of the green-tiled bathroom counter. He'd already moved in.

Jack didn't have a regular job. He stayed at home in blue boxer shorts, sipping Scotch and water from a cut crystal glass. His chest was smooth and hairless. He made produce deals on the telephone with growers in Yuma, Buckeye, El Centro, and Salinas, then worried if insects or the weather would ruin the crops. Once, I heard him bet $10,000 on a fighter named Zora Foley.

"I'd like to own a piece of him," he said.

I asked how he could buy part of someone.

He laughed. "With plenty of money." He told me that one night Zora Foley had taught him to play the bongo drums at a victory party in Las Vegas.

Jack was a big spender. He took us to the rodeo, a football game, and Disneyland. We ate out at Durant's, the Knotty Pines, and the Stockyards Restaurant, expensive steak houses where Jack knew the owners. We sat in dark red booths, ate shrimp cocktails, filet mignon, baked potatoes, and salad with Roquefort dressing.

Jack loved to cook. He wore a plaid apron and made things like a basted ham covered with a thick crust of cooked dough. His specialty was Chicken Marengo. He went hunting and brought home quail and other small birds to cook, covering them in sweet fruity sauces.

He bought us the horse he'd promised. We named her Honeybee, but she turned out to be a wild horse and couldn't be tamed. We never rode her. Jack bought Kimberly a trampoline. He taught me to dive by showing me how to double over and fall in. He took me to the record store to buy the top-ten hits, made jokes, asking the salesman if *he* had "Pretty Blue Eyes." My mother didn't like dogs, but Jack talked her into letting Kimberly and me have two Beagle puppies.

Late at night, I hid in the hallway and watched as they slow danced in the living room, his hand resting on the side of my mother's hip. When she did leg kicks in the swimming pool for slimmer thighs, Jack would sit on the edge near the ladder where she held on to steady herself, and said things that made her laugh. She hadn't laughed much with Ed. I didn't remember how she was with my real father.

I tried to resist him and all his gifts, but inside I felt an opening like a crack in the desert floor making a channel for rainwater.

After he made a produce deal, he and my mother would drive out to the fields in Buckeye or Yuma to check on the crops. In her short, brown leather boots, the bottoms of her tight-fitting blue jeans tucked in the tops, and a shirt with little silver snaps on the pockets, she'd say, "We're off to work." Out they'd go, ice clinking in their drinks, waving to us as they backed out of the driveway in the Lincoln. Hours later, they'd come home carrying heads of lettuce, cucumbers, or strawberries covered in mud.

One day, Jack took Kimberly and me along too. He checked in, speaking Spanish with the head field worker who stayed in a small trailer near one of the irrigation ditches. Then, while my mother stayed in the car, listening to Tony Bennett and drinking Bloody Mary's from a thermos, my sister and I followed Jack out into acreage of quiet, sweet smelling dirt. We walked behind him in our tooled leather cowboy boots, through labyrinths of butterball and romaine, as he looked for signs of whether or not his investment was going to pay off.

He wouldn't let us talk until after his inspection.

Bending down, close to the earth, he sniffed handfuls of irrigated soil. He searched for insects and stroked the underside of leaves, feeling with his fingers for the bugs that weren't visible.

I could feel the whole crop speaking to him through his hands. He seemed to know what it needed. It was the same way he patted meat when he barbequed hamburgers, as if he'd had a relationship with the animal, the way he lovingly cooked quail in golden-brown sauces, how he touched my mother's skin and sometimes put his hand on my shoulder when he made a joke, or lifted Kimberly up to ride on his shoulders.

As we walked through the butterball crop, Jack slipped a knife from the pocket of his loose-fitting pants, cut a piece of the vegetable from its roots, and chewed it. We walked some more. Then he stopped, lifted his head up, and peered at the sky from behind his black horn rim sunglasses.

"You can't control nature," he said. "If lettuce gets too

cold, the heads will be too small. If it's too hot, they'll wilt. And if the wind comes up, the heads could get windburn. It's a risky business."

When his assessment was complete, he let out a scream. We were scared at first.

"It releases tension," he said. "Where else can you scream and no one will hear you?"

I tried to imitate Jack, making the loudest noise I could, but I started to cough. The more I screamed though, the throat screeching stopped and I felt the sound coming from my whole body.

Jack taught us to make animal sounds. Kimberly liked to imitate birds. I preferred wild cats. Jack could become any animal we thought of. Our favorite was his imitation of an anteater. He stuck his tongue out, slithered it from side to side and made licking sounds.

As we walked back to the car, Jack taught us his rendition of "I'm An Old Cowhand From The Rio Grande" and we sang together, laughing.

*I'm an old cowpie*
*In the pasture I lie*
*Oh, my feet don't match*
*And my head needs a scratch.*
*Though my feet don't match*
*And my head needs a scratch*
*I'm still a cowpie*
*That'll get your ass*
*Yippie yi yo kayah*

"How does everything look?" my mother asked. She stood at the edge where the crops ended and the desert began.

Jack lit a cigarette and put his arm around her.

"So far, so good," he said.

\*\*\*

One day, two hulking men came to the door demanding to know Jack's whereabouts. He was in Salinas, but my mother told me not to tell them. She made me answer the door and say, "My parents aren't home." The men stood on the doorjamb, leaned forward into the house, close to me. I thought they would push me out of the way or put me in handcuffs. They looked like they had guns. My whole body trembled. I wanted to run, but I stood there trying to appear taller than I was. I kept saying, "They aren't here. They aren't here," until finally, they left.

"Who are those men?" I asked my mother.

"Friends of Jack's."

"They don't look like friends."

She went to her bedroom and closed the door. I heard sobbing that penetrated the walls of the house.

Later, she told Kimberly and me that Jack wasn't coming back. She was divorcing him, and we had to move out of state. She found out he'd been writing bad checks for a long time. He'd forged her signature, taken her inheritance money, and Kimberly's and my trust funds. He'd invested all of it on what turned out to be a bad crop of cucumbers.

I didn't know what a trust fund was, but if Jack had taken all our money he must have had a good reason. He had plans to legally adopt us, so he had to come home.

Kimberly wouldn't go in the pool without him. She started stealing. She'd race down Glendale Avenue to the Rexall Drug store, making the playing cards in the spokes of her bike spin until you couldn't see them. Her thin brown hair, separated into pigtails, looked like sprouting palm trees waving in the wind. She brought home bags of records, hair spray, make-up, candy, and comic books.

I told her Jack would be back any day, he just needed time to get some money together.

"Will he be the same as before?"

"He'll be better," I said.

The big men kept coming to the door, now asking for my mother. I tried to control the shaking in my body when I told them my parents weren't home. I felt like a criminal and wondered if they'd put me in handcuffs if they found out I was lying.

I thought my mother wanted Jack to come back, too, until the locksmith came. And then I heard her on the phone inviting a man over for dinner. She put lemon chicken in the oven. I tiptoed down the hall and peeked around the corner to see who it was. Bob Arden, owner of the Knotty Pines restaurant. We'd eaten there. We'd met him. He was a friend of Jack's. He and my mother were listening to Andy Williams and drinking martinis on the couch in the living room. The lights were low. I'd seen her replace the regular bulbs with pink ones before he arrived.

She leaned into him and put her bold red lips on his mouth.

I rushed to get Kimberly. She was watching the ballerina in her music box spin around to the "Blue Danube Waltz."

"Let's go out there and do a dance for them," I said. "That way, they can't kiss or anything."

"Does she still love Daddy?"

"Yes. But we have to keep an eye on her."

We got Cokes in the kitchen and went to the living room

in our petticoat dance outfits with our plan. Kimberly carried a little drum. I took a box of checkers as a back-up of something to do after our performance.

"What are you girls doing?" my mother said.

"We're here to dance for Mr. Arden."

"Aren't you cute," he said, sucking a martini-soaked olive into his mouth.

Kimberly tapped her drum, and the doorbell rang.

"Don't answer that," my mother said.

It rang again. We all stared at the front door.

Then we heard Jack's voice, thick and hoarse. "Gail, I know you're in there, and I know who you're with."

"It's Daddy," Kimberly said. She started for the door. I grabbed her arm and held her back.

"Bob, get the hell out of my house and away from my wife."

My mother froze like an ice sculpture, her arm raised with the martini glass in her hand, ready to drink.

"Daddy," Kimberly yelled.

The doorbell rang again and again. The checkers spilled at my feet and scattered across the carpet. I felt my stomach churn. The bones in my legs got soft. It was hard to keep standing.

"Bob! Gail! Answer the door or I'm breaking it down!"

I put my arm around Kimberly's small chest. I could feel her heart pounding.

She looked up at me. "He sounds real mad."

Jack kept yelling, "I'll break the door down!" Then we heard a gunshot. A bullet went through the front door and hit the wall that faced the entryway, blackening the woven linen wallpaper.

My mother dropped her glass and screamed.

Bob ran through the kitchen. I heard the back door slam.

*What a coward*, I thought.

"I'm going to call the police," I yelled out.

"No," said Kimberly. "They'll take him away."

"He's going to kill someone."

I dragged Kimberly with me to the kitchen and dialed the phone. "Come to 708 North Third Avenue. My father shot a gun."

Jack yelled, "Dreams. You've taken them all away, Gail."

Then we heard pounding, wood splitting, cracking, as part of the door collapsed.

Jack stepped into the living room in a wrinkled shirt and pants, his shoes caked with dried mud.

"Daddy," Kimberly cried.

"I brought this lettuce for you and the girls," he said. "This is a good crop. The cucumbers weren't my fault. It was the beetles. They ate the seedlings."

Weaving back and forth, holding a head of dirty lettuce in one hand and the gun in the other, he kicked a heavy cardboard box of butterball into the room and walked toward my mother, throwing the head of lettuce at her.

I didn't think he would shoot Kimberly, or me, but my mother could be dead before the police came. I couldn't think of what to do. My body took over. I pushed Kimberly behind me and walked forward until I stood between Jack and my mother. My bravery surprised me.

"Aren't you a big deal," I said. My heart cracked in crooked pieces. "I was right about you in the beginning."

He dropped the gun to his side, made a low howling sound, turned and walked away into the night toward an old beat-up car parked across the street.

The police finally came and asked my mother all kinds of questions.

"Was he drunk? Are you still married? Did he hit the girls? Did he hit you?"

"I want a restraining order," my mother said.

After they left, it was quiet except for Andy Williams, who'd been singing the "Hawaiian Wedding Song" for hours. The arm of the record player kept lifting up and gliding over the record until the needle dropped down to that last song on the album.

My mother's lemon chicken burned up in the oven, first flesh, then bones. It smoked its way through the house. We breathed it all in: dead chicken, shattered plaster, Tangueray gin, and gunmetal.

# Alligator Dreams

When my mother and Jack were still married, I overheard them one night talking about adopting a baby boy, and that he was coming to our house for a trial run. Jack said, "It'd be so perfect to raise a child with you." *What about Kimberly and me?* I thought. I didn't want a brother, especially an adopted one. I knew my sister and I had to do something to make sure they sent him back. They hadn't even consulted us. Besides, Jack, who we'd just started calling "Daddy" and using his last name in preparation for our legal adoption (Kimberly had secretly carved her new initials into the backseat of the new Cadillac he'd bought) already had a real daughter, not step, from another marriage, and we'd had to share him and our trip to Disneyland with her. We didn't need any more siblings.

I told Kimberly the baby would get all their attention. She was two years younger and truth eluded her, as it did my mother. After three attempts at marriage, my mother believed she'd finally gotten it right with Jack. I'd hoped so too.

The first night the baby arrived—and Kimberly saw Jack and my mother dancing around the kitchen, passing him back and forth, laughing, making goo goo ga ga noises, completely ignoring us—she got the picture. "They didn't even make dinner," she said.

The baby was an ugly color of red, and he cried too much. My mother tried not to show it, but I could tell his sounds annoyed her. Kimberly and I decided that if we could get him to cry more, it would push my mother over the edge, and that would be the end of him.

We met every day after school under a tent of blankets Kimberly had built in her room. We thought of obvious things we'd seen on TV, like tying him up or putting a pillow over his face, just enough to cause more crying, but we didn't want to accidentally kill him.

One night, Jack took us to dinner at The Stockyards, his favorite restaurant. Kimberly and I ordered shrimp cocktails as an appetizer. With tiny forks, we dipped orange striped bodies into cocktail sauce, watching my mother and Jack dote on the baby in his highchair. We looked at each other and then at our forks, and we knew we had our answer.

The next day, under the tent, we worked out our strategy. We would each carry a shrimp fork with us at all times, and when no one was looking, take turns poking the baby's feet, not hard enough to hurt him, just enough to make him fussy. We did it when he was in his high chair, in his crib and when we rode with him in the back seat of the car.

The day the adoption people took him away, Kimberly and I hugged each other and ate Hostess cupcakes under the tent to celebrate our success

Later, I overheard my mother talking with Jack about whether or not she should have surgery to correct her tipped uterus, which is why she couldn't get pregnant.

The doctor said it must have tilted backwards when she gave birth to Kimberly.

"It'd be worth it," Jack said. "The child would be a complete expression of us. If it doesn't work, we can always try another baby to adopt."

"It's all too much." My mother's voice rose higher. She'd had it. I heard a glass smash on the kitchen floor.

Jack stayed for another year; and in that time, my mother didn't have surgery and no other baby came to our house.

Soon after he left, my mother made plans to leave Arizona. In the divorce, she would have been responsible for all the debt Jack had run up. She moved us to Florida, a non-community property state.

\*\*\*

My sister and I watched her through a crack in our bedroom door. My mother sat at the fake wood dining table in her bra and girdle, a bottle of vodka in front of her, writing letters in large, insistent printing. The light fixture hanging from the ceiling, its dusty frosted bulbs curved at the tip, lit her words. Her gold and ivory pillbox with the Greek statues on top, full of Dexemil, sat open on the table next to the vodka. "Stranger on the Shore" played from the living room. Jack had sent her the record to let her know how he felt.

Kimberly and I were waiting for our Meals on Wheels dinners to be delivered: little foil tubs of eggplant or chicken or some kind of meat, all smothered in the same red sauce. My mother had stopped cooking, and we didn't know how.

"She's so disgusting," Kimberly said. "Who is she writing to anyway?"

"Jack. She still loves him."

My mother's thin, paper skin legs crossed at the knees and again at the ankles. Her foot pumped up and down. Her toes, like ten red shiny snake eyes, flashed back at us from across the room.

"Have you noticed, the more she drinks, the more her legs squeeze together?" I said.

"Girls, are you doing your homework?"

"Watch her mouth," Kimberly whispered. "See how loose it gets."

The more she drank, my mother's gestures—smoking, writing, gulping vodka—became more animated. Her pen bore down harder. She mouthed the words she wrote.

"How does she cross her legs like that?" I said.

Kimberly, who had inherited the same skinny legs, wound hers around each other in imitation. We laughed.

"Linda. Kimberly. Did you do the laundry?" Her words slurred. We didn't answer. The meal truck pulled up outside.

"Girls, your dinners are here."

The deliveryman left them on the doormat. We carried them in and ate in our room, sitting side by side on my twin bed, balancing aluminum trays on our laps. There wasn't room at the dining table.

When she thought we were asleep, my mother snuck into our bedroom (we hadn't shared a room since we were small) and kissed us, then cried, making eerie sounds like a ghost. In the morning, she seemed numb and weary as she dressed for work and applied make-up to her puffy face. Envelopes peeked out from her purse, ready to mail.

\*\*\*

When we moved to Florida, I was fourteen, Kimberly, twelve. My mother told us we had to grow up now and stop calling her "Mommy." She didn't like "Mom" so we were instructed to only call her "Mother." I couldn't get used to the change so I didn't call her anything for six months.

That summer, Kimberly and I rode with her from our apartment in the crummy part of Fort Lauderdale to Saks Fifth Avenue where she'd gotten her first job. The store was near the beach. She dropped us off near the Elbo Room, where college kids came for spring break.

My sister and I wore bikinis with huge wooden Tiki gods around our necks like we'd seen on other girls. We'd share a box of frozen chocolate éclairs for breakfast and spread our Arizona desert bodies out into the thick muggy air, under the cloudy light of the Florida sun.

We hadn't seen sailors before, except on TV. Here, they walked on the beach in their uniforms and tried to pick us up. None of them were cute; most had bad acne and they scared us. They came too close, stepped on the edge of our towels, leaving a mark and a mound of sand. We made a plan that when they approached us—we'd speak in a made-up language. "Hiya girls," they'd say. "Shamick lipnapana," Kimberly said. "You girls German or some-thing?" "Maneek manula kapo," I said. We shook our heads, "Michsmashna shimisna?" They walked away, crunching sand with their heavy black shoes. We laughed and ate another éclair.

My mother dated an assortment of men: Sylvan Rice, a jewelry buyer from Miami, carried a poodle under his arm and had white hair and a skinny silver line of stubble across his upper lip; Jim Brown, a former race car driver; Libertis Van Bocklin, one of the Ladies Shoes salesmen from Saks; a short tan internist who owned a sailboat; and some Italian guy who didn't want to have anything to do with children. My mother proudly showed Kimberly and me the pink and gold leaf Limoges perfume tray the Italian brought her from Paris.

She took trips with her boyfriends. We'd come home from school on Friday and there would be a note saying she'd be gone for the weekend. Or we'd receive a postcard in the mail on Monday after she'd already come home and gone back to work.

During the holidays, I wrapped Christmas gifts at Saks; and Kimberly once modeled a new haircut created by a famous Spanish hairdresser who visited the Saks Beauty Salon.

My mother taught us how to make cheap clothes look expensive. This worked best with anything black.

When school started, Kimberly and I tried to figure out how to fit in with the hoodlums—girls with pale lipstick and ratted beehive hair holding little clip-on bows; boys with big greasy pompadour hair and cigarette packs rolled up in T-shirt sleeves at the top of their pale arms. We'd never met kids like this, only seen them on TV. We were accepted when we copied how they looked, started smoking, and said "fuck" a lot.

After a year, my mother said she couldn't support both of us on her salesgirl's salary and that I would have to go back to Phoenix and live with my grandmother until I graduated from high school.

"No way," I said. "I won't go."

"We can quit school and go to work," Kimberly said.

"Why can't she just send money?" I asked.

"Don't worry. It's temporary. When your grandmother

dies, we'll have money again, and then we can do whatever we want."

Kimberly's shoulders rolled forward and rose up to her ears. Her eyes opened wide.

"Kimberly has to go too," I said.

"Grandma will only take you. You know you're her favorite."

"It's not fair," I said. "You want to get rid of me."

Kimberly ran to the bedroom and slammed the door.

I pounded my fist on the table, spilling my mother's glass of vodka. "I won't go!"

She jumped up, stood behind her chair, arms crossed. "We have to be realistic. You can come home for Christmas and summers. Did you hear that, Kimberly?"

Alone in our room, my sister choked on her sobs. "I can't stay here without you."

"I'll talk Grandma into letting you come too," I said with certainty, though I knew that would probably never happen.

That night, in the swampy darkness, our separation began as we lay in our twin beds, awake, backs curled away from each other, too numb to speak. I missed her already.

\*\*\*

*Dear Linda,*

*I caught Mother and Jimmie, that cousin of hers, who she continues to believe is going to help her out financially, naked on the living room floor. They were asleep. It was two in the morning on Friday night. I got up to get a glass of water and saw them. She didn't have her wig on. She's been wearing wigs lately so she doesn't have to curl her hair. I thought I was seeing things. You know how when you walk in the dark you* have to adjust your eyes? I knew they'd been fucking. I went back to my room and started laughing hysterically and then I started to cry. I waited a while and went out there again. He was gone. I saw her wig on top of the TV with a fifty dollar bill on it. Can you believe it? She's so disgusting.

On Saturday there was a marathon dance contest at Kmart. I was gone for two days. When I came home, she started screaming at me. I told her I knew about her and Jimmie. She called me a liar with a big imagination.

I told my friend Pat about it, and she told her mother. Pat's mother said that when women get divorced they want sex all the time because they're used to having it. I asked Mother if this was the deal with her. She told me I was crazy. She said it was too bad we had to live in a neighborhood with ignorant, uneducated people.

I won the dance contest; but I couldn't collect the prize money cause I'm under age, and I entered illegally. The final song was "Fingertips." It was so fun. I didn't even get tired. Afterwards, we all went to a construction site and had a drinking party. The cops picked us up. At the police station, everyone's parents were called to come and get their kids. Mother was the only one they couldn't reach. So the cop drove me home. There was a note on the door. She was out of town for the weekend. She's hardly ever home anymore. The cop was shocked. I realized for the first time that there is something very wrong with our mother.

I wrote to Daddy, well, Jack. I don't know what to call him anymore. Mother wouldn't give me his address. She mailed it for me. He wrote back saying he'd been busy with his produce business selling onions and radishes. He hoped I was getting good grades at school so I could go to college. He made a joke asking if my pet turtles went swimming with me in the ocean. He must think I'm still ten years old. He signed it, "All my *love, Daddy." The postmark is from Phoenix so he must still be there. Maybe you'll see him.*

*Do you like living with Grandma? Did you talk to her about me? Are you still coming home for Christmas? I hate being here by myself.*

*One of mother's boyfriends bought me a parakeet. I named him Theodore Oglethorpe Lange.*

*Love from your baby sister,*
*Kimberly (K)*

*P.S. I have a boyfriend. His name is Butch Balla. He's a dropout, but I don't care. He's really cool. He's a drummer. I'm changing my name to the letter K, so call me that from now on. K? HA! HA! HA!*

*Dear K,*

*I like Kimberly better, but I'll try to remember to call you K. Stay away from that creep, Jimmie. Don't ever see him by yourself. Remember that time he took me out on his sailboat? Well, he tried all kinds of things. Yuck! Talk about disgusting. I wanted to call you, but Grandma won't let me make long distance calls. Remember Patty, my friend at Northeast High? Do you ever see her? She wrote me a letter and told me she got pregnant. She had an abortion. I called her and when the operator asked for my number, I gave her a made up one instead of Grandma's. Well, I got caught and Grandma took the phone out of my room and hid it in the attic. Anyway, Patty's all right but she was really scared. Her parents never found out. Be careful. Don't get pregnant!*

*Grandma caught me smoking but didn't say much about it. She smokes a lot. And boy does she drink! I have to do all* these chores. She said something about earning my keep. She writes down every penny she spends on me, even gum, in a black ledger book.

This morning she gave me vacuuming lessons. She does it in the nude. So disgusting! She made me check all the Roach Motels. I found a dead one, and she seemed to want to celebrate. She fixed oatmeal for breakfast and decided there were bugs in it, spooned out a glob and brought it right in my face with a magnifying glass. "See those little rascals," she said. "There's part of a wing and a leg." I didn't see anything. I think she was hallucinating. But I'm never eating oatmeal again. When I try to help her in the kitchen she pushes me out of the way with her elbow. I get the feeling she's wanted to push someone around for a long time.

She has all this money, but she saves everything. She washes out paper towels and dental floss and uses them over again and she hasn't bought any clothes for years. She showed me where she keeps Grandpa's ashes on a shelf in the closet. I wish you were here.

I made a friend at school. Her name is Arlene. She made fake IDs and we went to the Playboy Club to apply for jobs as Bunnies, to see what it was like. The Bunny mother who was pretty old had us try on that strapless bodysuit, rabbit ears and fluffy tail. It was so tight, your butt hangs out and it's made out of cheap satin. She taught us the Bunny Dip. I couldn't do it. You have to bend your knees and lean way back while holding a tray and serve drinks so the men can't see down your top even though your boobs are pushed up and almost hanging out of your Bunny suit. It's ridiculous! The Bunnies make a lot of money. Arlene thinks maybe she'll go back when she graduates. I don't know what I'll do, but there has to be a better way for a woman to make money.

Arlene is cool, though. She has a driver's license and a car.

*On Friday and Saturday nights, she drives me to Baboquiv-
ari's in Scottsdale, a beatnik coffee house that has folk music
and an open mic, so I can read my poetry. The entertainment
takes place on a wooden porch under huge cottonwood trees.
I dress in black and my bleached hair is down to my waist
now. It's a cool place, named after Baboquivari Peak, a sacred
mountain for native people. At the end, people snap their
fingers instead of clapping. I'm going to find out if I can hang
my art there.*

*I thought I saw Jack Lange the other day when Grandma
and I went to the grocery store. There was a man across the
street that looked like him. He had the same kind of glasses,
but this guy was a bum. Calling him by his full name feels
right because he doesn't seem like someone we knew very well,
after all.*

*I guess being here is better than living with Mother. At
least the house is big. I'm waiting for the right time to talk to
Grandma about you living here. There's plenty of room, but
I think she's having a hard time getting used to me. In the
meantime, maybe she'll let you come for a visit. I miss you.
I'll see you in a couple of months. We can go to the beach.
Maneek manula kapo. HA! HA!*

*Love from your big sister,
Linda
xoxoxoxox*

***

Christmas was coming. I'd never been away from my
mother and sister during the holidays, but my grandmother wouldn't buy me a plane ticket.

"I'll pay for the bus," she said.

"Across the country? How long will that take? What

about sleeping and eating? What kind of people will be on the bus?" I imagined having to protect myself from being robbed, raped, or killed. My stomach knotted up at the thought. How would I manage? I was fourteen, but at six feet tall, I looked much older. Maybe that would help.

"You'll be fine," my grandmother said, handing me two checks for five dollars each, one made out to me, the other to Kimberly. Her usual Christmas gift to us.

***

In the boarding area, harsh yellow spotlights beamed through heavy cigarette smoke, blocking out a shiny black sky. The bus driver—his shirt said Earl—picked up my suitcase with his thin-boned arm and put it in a compartment under the bus.

"You and your belongings is safe with me, little lady. Pick you out a seat by a window. Best way to see America."

The smoky bus was half-full. A woman kept a baby wrapped in a shawl tight against her chest. One man held a huge pink teddy bear; another, wearing a jean suit, sang "I Left My Heart in San Francisco."

I sat behind Earl. He started the bus. The door closed with a sucking sound. It was pitch dark except for tiny red lights on the floor and the ones on the dashboard that made a dull glow on Earl's cheekbones. We pulled away from the Phoenix depot, passed the neon blue BUS sign flanked by two leaping greyhounds, the Standard Brands paint store, and the Trade Winds Bar that promised the sexiest topless go-go dancers downtown. I lit a cigarette. Saguaros rose up under bright stars and a crescent moon. I shoved my purse full of cookies and snacks against the windowpane, leaned my head on it, and curled my body toward the landscape. It would be a long four days to Florida.

By the time we stopped in Abilene, I was hungry for something substantial. There was a dingy restaurant in the depot. Gawking men watched me as I ate chili, a sandwich with unrecognizable meat, and a slice of multi-fruit pie that looked like plastic, all of which exploded in my guts an hour later in the bathroom at the back of the bus as we rolled along through Texas farm land.

In Houston, I said goodbye to Earl. "Good luck, little lady," he said. The new driver licked his lips with a creepy smile. I changed my seat to one in the middle of the bus.

Biloxi was my favorite place. Weeping willows lined the water's edge. I wanted to lie down under their long, drooping branches. They were as strange and mysterious as saguaros, but as the willows moved gracefully, I imagined lying under them, safe from harm. I missed them as soon as the last one disappeared from sight. Kimberly would have loved them too. I wished she were with me. We could get off the bus anyplace we liked and start a new life.

In Mobile, Alabama, a black man got on, holding a pint of whiskey. He walked with a tired swagger, his body slightly slumped over. He sat down next to me. I heard my mother's voice telling me to be afraid, but I wasn't. He had a gaunt face with a goatee and two deep creases between his unruly, partially gray eyebrows. He asked me for a cigarette and offered me a swig. My grandmother had recently taught me that to avoid getting too drunk, it was best to drink straight liquor. "Don't mix it with anything or you'll get sick," she'd said after I'd gone to a party, had too many Screwdrivers, and vomited all night.

"Buddy," he said and shook my hand.

"Linda."

He said he made a living traveling the country betting on

horses. He thought his luck would change if he switched it up and bet on the dogs at Hollywood Park.

"Where's that?"

"Near the Everglades. There's magic there. Hey, what's a girl like you doin' riding the dog, anyway? You runnin' from somethin'?"

I told him I'd been living in Phoenix with my grandmother and was going home for Christmas. "Maybe my mother's found a rich boyfriend. Then I could live with her and my sister again. But my grandmother says my mother makes bad choices in men, so I probably wouldn't like him."

"Don't you worry, Miss Linda. Someday things'll change. All the old rich white men in power'll be dead."

In Tallahassee, Buddy transferred to another bus. "Good luck, missy. I'll make a bet on the dogs for you."

*\*\*\**

When I arrived in Fort Lauderdale, my ankles were swollen as big as my calves from sitting so long in a cramped seat. Exhausted, I'd been afraid to sleep on the bus. But I perked up as soon as I saw my mother.

"You made it," she said, with a tense smile. She gave me a thin hug. "I can't believe you came all this way on a bus."

"What choice did I have?"

"How was it?"

"Horrible."

"Well, you're here now. I have to hurry and change my clothes. I'm meeting my date in half an hour."

"You don't seem glad to see me."

"How can you say that? Of course I am." She rubbed her hand quickly over my back. "It feels like you've gained weight. We'll talk about everything tomorrow."

My mother had moved to a smaller apartment near a rib restaurant, a population of alligators conveniently farmed in the back.

Kimberly looked older than her twelve years. She'd grown as tall as I. Her skin was tanned like a chestnut. She wore thick, black eyeliner circling her hardened blue eyes, ratted beehive hair, and heavy white lipstick on her unsmiling mouth. I imagined a switchblade in her pocket. I hugged her. She didn't hug back. There was no give in her body, except for the soft tiny pat of her hand on my back.

"My bird, Theodore, died. I had to bury him," she said, releasing herself from me.

"How'd he die?"

"I don't want to talk about it." She lit a cigarette. "Will you trim my bangs?"

A crooked aluminum Christmas tree sat on a wrought iron table. I didn't recognize the furniture. It belonged outside by a swimming pool.

Kimberly turned one of the patio chairs from the dining table around toward the kitchen, went in the bathroom and came out with a pair of scissors and a hand mirror, a striped beach towel hanging over her shoulders.

"So how is it living with Grandma?"

"I'm sorry she wouldn't let you come. It's not great."

"At least you have some money."

"Not really. I have to steal clothes because she won't buy me any."

"Me too."

"I'm doing this vertically so it won't be too even."

"Let me see."

I gave her the hand mirror. She checked her bangs then

tilted the mirror up slightly to look at me. Her eyes were like hard rockets, with lids like a reptile.

"You may continue," she said.

"Yes, madam. It looks good. Want to go to the beach tomorrow? We could get a box of éclairs."

"I'll be with Butch."

"He could come too."

She laughed.

A horn honked outside. Kimberly threw off the beach towel, ran out the door, and yelled, "Thanks. That's my boyfriend, Butch. See ya later."

I wanted to use the scissors on my mother.

I didn't see Kimberly later. I hardly saw my mother or Kimberly during my visit. My sister and I opened gifts together on Christmas morning, sitting by the fake tree in our baby-doll pajamas. Two each, wrapped in Saks Fifth Avenue's gold and white-striped paper, tied with red ribbon. They were the same: a bottle of White Shoulder's spray cologne and two pairs of white bikini panties.

"She used her thirty percent employee discount on this stuff," Kimberly said.

"Where is she anyway?"

"Where she always is, out with some guy."

"I wish we could go back to the way things were with Jack."

Kimberly lit a cigarette. "Those are the breaks, I guess."

"Things have to get better sometime, don't you think?"

"No."

My mother came through the front door wearing a disheveled smile. "Girls, guess what? Cousin Jimmie has invited us to Christmas brunch at the Bahia Mar. Let's get dressed."

I wanted to throw up.

"No way," said Kimberly.

"You go, Mother. We'll stay here."

"I think you're being very ungrateful, but have it your way."

After my mother left, Kimberly got dressed and patted me on the shoulder before she went out, signaled once again by Butch's honking horn.

I cried and drank vodka until I passed out on the couch.

The next day, despite having followed my grandmother's rule to only drink straight liquor, I was hungover. I walked to the alligator farm a few blocks away. The smell of alligator meat wafted through our apartment at dinnertime. I returned every day to watch the baby alligators ride around on their mother's snouts.

On my last morning, my mother stayed in her bedroom. She'd left a can of mace, money for the cab ride to the bus depot, and a note on the kitchen table saying, "*See heaven by looking down.* A quote from Shakespeare." This was her attempt to communicate something meaningful to me. If I could find which play the quote came from, maybe I could figure out what she was trying to tell me.

Before the cab came, I slammed cupboards, cleared my throat, turned on the radio, in case she was really asleep and I could wake her. I tested her bedroom door. It was locked. I put my ear against the fake wood. Was she with a man? I couldn't hear a sound.

I walked down the hall to Kimberly's room. It smelled of cheap hairspray and pot. There were piles of clothes on the floor, rumpled bed sheets, and streaks of make-up on the pillows. Spread out on the dresser, among a mess of uncapped eyeliner pencils, I saw my new lipstick and the silver hoop earrings I'd bought on sale at Britt's department store. She'd taken them from my purse. There were dusty seashells of many shapes and colors, the ones we collected last summer on the beach. I picked up the smallest one with the pale orange spirals and slipped it into my pocket.

I went back to the kitchen. There was a box of chocolate éclairs on the counter I hadn't noticed earlier. I was leaving her alone again, this time with Butch, the hoodlum, and the smell of grilling alligator meat smoking through the apartment.

***

On the way back to Phoenix, the bus stopped in Baton Rouge. As I walked to the vending machines, a detective grabbed my arm, showed me his badge and a picture of a girl who looked like me kneeling beside a big black poodle in a snowy yard. "No more running, Susie, come with me."

"That's not me. Where are you taking me?" I clenched my jaw and looked around for possible exits. "My name isn't Susie." I tried to pull away.

"How old are you?"

"None of your business. I'm on my way to Phoenix."

He made me stand with him at the pay phone while he called my grandmother.

He finally let me go.

I pushed on his chest. "You shouldn't grab people."

Later, I wondered what had made Susie run.

In Sweetwater, Texas, a blonde woman, with bouffant hair and heavy make-up got on the bus and sat down next to me. Her pink dress was too tight, showed so much cleavage it was hard not to stare, and she wore a sickening rose fragrance. She said she was on her way to Juarez, Mexico where she lived out in the country on a ranch with a group of girls like me who'd run away from unhappy homes—girls with incestuous fathers and raging, abusive mothers.

"Why does everyone think I'm a runaway?"

"Oh, darlin', it's obvious you're not happy."

She was the only person who'd noticed, so I told her about Jack stealing my mother's money, my sister who'd become a delinquent, and that I had nowhere to go after high school.

"You can live with me and the other girls on the ranch."

"But I want to go to art school."

She smiled and put her wrinkled, ring-bedecked hand over mine. "Sweetie, after a year or two working at the ranch, you'll have plenty of money for art school."

"What would I do there?"

"Don't worry about that. I'll teach you everything you need to know."

"Like what?"

"Do you like boys?" She slid her bracelets up and down her arm. "Maybe your sister would like to come too. Do you have a picture of her?"

I showed her one I'd taken of Kimberly standing in front of the apartment building with her neatly trimmed bangs, in cut-off jeans, smoking, with her lip in a snarl.

"She's cute, but you're perfect," the woman said. "You have that pouty, sensuous, flat-tummied, long look."

I rubbed the back of my neck. My mouth was dry.

"What do you say about coming with me?"

"I don't know."

"Think about it." She got up, smoothed her dress, and went to the bathroom.

Minutes later, we stopped in El Paso. She said she had to transfer to another bus to go across the border.

"Sure you don't want to come along?"

I cleared my throat. "I don't think I'm ready."

She handed me her card embossed with a picture of a beautiful Spanish ranch house. It said *Sylvia* with a phone number at the bottom.

"Call me when you decide you want to be happy." She turned and waved as she left.

\*\*\*

The next day, sitting at the kitchen table, I told my grandmother I'd had a job offer.

"Oh, honey. That's wonderful." She was standing at the counter, downing shots of bourbon and making lunch: sardine and onion sandwiches on black bread. I wanted to shock her, make her protective, but I knew that was futile.

I gazed out the window, got lost in the milky blue sky. My time here was running out. Where would I go after graduation? All I wanted was to lie down in the backyard and hide forever under the fragrant, low hanging, white blossoms of my grandmother's magnolia tree.

That night, I dreamed of being chased by alligators with very fast legs. They vanished into a white mist right before they wrestled me to the ground, their teeth ready to clamp down on my flesh.

\*\*\*

*Dear Linda,*

*I don't know if Mother told you I was arrested and went to juvenile jail for supposedly stealing her car and jewelry. I wanted you to know the truth. I only borrowed her car for a trip to New Orleans with my friend, Pat. I didn't have* my license yet, but Mother's boyfriend, Jim Brown, gave me driving lessons. Did you ever meet him? He used to be a race car driver. When we got to New Orleans, two guys, hitch-hikers we'd picked up, stole the car from us. And Butch was the one who stole Mother's jewelry. But Mother doesn't care about the truth.

Now I'm in Batesburg, South Carolina at a school for bad girls called St. Euphrasia. I wasn't allowed to write to you from jail 'cause I tried to escape and got caught. That place was a real bummer. How could they put a thirteen- year-old in jail? The barbed wire fence was really high. I didn't expect so many bars on the windows.

My jail outfit was a baggy gray dress. I wondered if the girl who wore it before me was a murderer.

At first, I was in a cell alone and wasn't allowed to go outside. I played the good girl and finally got a roommate. Nelda was from Jacksonville, in for robbery. We started plan-ning our escape. We practiced jumping from the floor, tried to get as high as the top bunk bed so we'd be in shape to get over the barbed wire fence when they let us go outside.

Remember when you used to practice flying, how you'd stand at the back of the patio, run fast, and jump up and out as far as you could? I told Nelda in order to get distance, the jumping had to be an up and out kind of thing. That way, when we got close to the fence we wouldn't have to start at the bottom and climb up. We could leap up onto it and scramble across before the guards could catch us.

The first day they let us outside for exercise we did a hundred jackknives before it started to rain. The guards were caught by surprise and got upset about getting wet. Nelda and I looked at each other. We knew this was our chance. We ran across the yard, slammed into the fence, crawled fast, like spiders spread *out on a web, our hands and feet gripping link after link, reaching higher and higher.*

*Nelda got over first. I got caught at the top with my thigh stuck on one of the wires. A guard tried to pull me down, making a gash in my leg. I kicked her. Nelda helped pull me over. We jumped to the ground and ran through water and mud toward a parking lot. We searched for a car with keys in it. Then we heard sirens and headed for a ditch to hide in. A cop came out of nowhere and caught Nelda. I grabbed a rock. I came up behind him to hit him in the head, but he turned around and saw me. I dropped the rock fast and said, "Oh, hi." I don't know why I said that!*

*Then more cops came and handcuffed us. On the way back to jail, I was shocked to see roadblocks had been set up, just to find us, like on TV. We were muddy and soaking wet. My leg was bleeding. Later, when I took a shower, a guard came in and hit me thirty times with a belt. It really hurt!*

*At my hearing, the judge read the charges against me. I was shocked. I had no idea I'd broken all those laws—truancy, grand theft, attempted assault of a police officer. The judge gave me a choice of going to the state juvenile jail or to St. Euphrasia for a year. Did Grandma tell you she agreed to pay for it? You know how she's always thought I was brain damaged from being born premature. I think that's why she decided to pay. The judge said I was lucky.*

*The whole time I was in jail, I wanted to kill myself. But not anymore. I love it here. I wish I could stay forever. The nuns are great. Mother Eugenia is my favorite. She's teaching me self-respect, discipline, and faith in God. I do a lot of singing in the chapel. God is love!*

*When I leave here, I'll have to live with Mother. Yuck! It will be temporary, but I have to have a place to go before they let me out. I'm thinking I could get a job working in a zoo.*

*That would be neat. Don't you think? I'd probably have to get my GED, though.*

*Anyway, write soon. The nuns don't confiscate letters. GOD BLESS YOU!*

*Love from your baby sister,*
*Kimberly Ann*
*(I'm not going by K anymore)*

*P.S. I hope you like the bookmarks. I picked the ones I thought had the best artwork. My favorite is St. Francis holding the animals.*

*Dear Kimberly Ann,*

*Every time I talk to Mother, she sobs and tells me how you've ruined her life. It makes me sick. I feel like beating her up. She's such a bitch. She's the one who ruined everything! I'm sorry I left you alone with her and that you've had such a horrible time. But maybe St. Euphrasia is the perfect place to get things started on a better path. We can't give up hope. Isn't it against the law for a guard to beat someone in the shower? Maybe you could sue the state or something.*

*I wrote a letter to the jail, but they must have confiscated it. I'm glad you like the nuns, and I hope they can help you get what you need. I'm graduating next month. I wish you could be here. I won't have any family there. Grandma says she's too old to go out at night. I don't know where I'll go after graduation. Grandma is ready for me to move out. Write me again soon.*

*Love,*
*Linda*

\*\*\*

It took three years, but when her divorce from Jack was finalized and the money problems he'd caused were resolved, my mother moved from Fort Lauderdale, back to Phoenix. She and I moved into a two-bedroom in the beige, monstrous, ragged looking Orangewood apartment complex. There was nothing orange in sight, not even an orange tree. My mother had acquired experience working in the retail business and was hired as the manager of the sportswear department at Saks.

One day, Jack showed up at the apartment. Wrinkly lines covered his face. His sunglasses were held together on one side with a little piece of tape. His filmy shirt stuck to his body with big sweat marks under his arms. He held a grocery bag from Bayless Market.

"Hi, honey. I didn't expect to see you. I thought you still lived with your grandmother." He reached out to hug me, and I pulled back. "Is your mother here?"

His hair stuck up straight, like before, but now it was in clumps like a dehydrated cat. Swamped with conflicted feelings, I wanted to scream, "Daddy, you're back," and then beat him up for ruining our lives.

"Mother's at work."

"She told me she didn't start until next week."

"They called her in early. I didn't know she talked to you."

I'd grown tall enough to meet him at eye level, but I couldn't look at him directly. I rounded my upper back, pulled my shoulders forward, and hung my head down, holding my breath tight against my ribs. It took all my strength to stop the waves of sadness from spinning out of my bones.

Jack shifted from one foot to the other. As his body

rocked, I noticed what looked like a coffee stain, the size of a pea, near the top button of his shirt. More than anything, I still wanted to be his daughter. I invited him in.

"Nice place," he said.

"You have to be kidding. What's in the bag?"

"Steaks and lettuce. I thought I'd cook for your mother. Are you hungry?"

"I'll put it in the fridge."

He sat on one end of the linen-covered couch my grandmother had given us.

"How's Kimberly?"

I sat across from him on the other side of the coffee table. "I haven't seen her for more than two years. She's locked up in that nun's place, scrubbing floors and singing hymns."

"I'd like to write to her. Does your mother have any cigarettes?"

"I do," I said and handed him one from the pack. "Would you like some water?"

"Do you have anything stronger?" He smiled.

The space between his teeth still showed when he grinned, but it took longer than I remembered for his smile to rise to his lips.

"Mother has vodka and wine. I have beer."

"That would be good. You have your own beer?"

"What about it?"

"Nothing. I wondered how you bought it, being underage."

"I have my ways." I went to the kitchen.

"So, what are you plans, honey?"

"I wish you wouldn't call me that. Plans?"

"Like college." He took a deep drag. "You have to think

about a career. Your mother tells me you're still interested in art."

"Yeah, right. You promised to send me to art school."

"I know I did, sweetie. That's why I came here today, to talk to your mother about the future."

What future? After everything he'd put her through, why had she talked to him? For years, I'd wondered if Jack had only been with us because my mother had money, and he'd planned to steal it from the beginning. As a child, I'd seen love between them, but I would never know for sure.

He twisted the shiny saw-toothed watchband on his left wrist, said he had a produce deal in the works, a big one that would pay off in the next few months, once the weather got warmer; after that, he'd make up for everything.

"Is it cucumbers again?"

He laughed. "In my line of work, there are down times. It can't be helped. Maybe we could get that house in Moon Valley you liked so much. Remember that bedroom with the window seat?"

"I'm sure it's not for sale after all these years." I crossed my legs and drank more beer.

"You never know. Is your mother seeing anyone?"

I told him about Carl. "She met him at Joe Hunt's bar. He's an industrial laundry machine salesman. Have you ever heard of such a thing? He wears a ruby pinky ring and red and yellow alpaca sweaters. He'll tell you what a great golfer he is. Mother thinks he looks like a cross between Jack Nicholson and Jack Nicklaus. I don't like him. Will you take me to the dog pound? I've been wanting to get a dog."

"Sure," he said with a big grin.

I don't know why I asked him. In some fractured way, I

wanted to recreate what I believed we once had, a family complete with a pet.

As we walked to his car, I noticed the heels of his shoes were worn down on the inside of the left foot and the outside of the right, like he was walking in two different directions. The old, beat-up car didn't have air conditioning. He said he was waiting for the new Cadillac convertible he'd ordered with leather seats and an eight-track tape deck. He drove with one hand at the top of the steering wheel, the bottle of beer between his legs.

"I saw a great movie. *Doctor Zhivago*. It's a love story written by a Russian named Boris Pasternak. It reminded me of your mother and me."

"Really?"

"Do you want a girl or a boy?"

"What?"

"Puppy."

"I don't know."

The pound smelled of urine and Clorox. I spotted the dog I wanted right away. He was the only puppy who didn't come running, hoping we'd save him. He stayed back and stared at us. He had long silky fur, three colors of brown, black, and white streaked together. After the other dogs calmed down, he walked over and licked Jack's pants through a space in the fence. Jack knelt down and petted his head. The woman in charge said he was mostly a mutt but had some Australian sheep dog in him.

He sat on my lap in the car, his paws on the edge of the open window, ears blown back, smiling at his good fortune. I decided to name him Boris, after the Russian. Jack stopped and bought dog food on the way back to the Orangewood. He said he had an appointment and had to run.

"I'll be back tomorrow, sweetie."

Boris and I waved goodbye.

I didn't see Jack again.

Later, my mother told me the last time she saw him was in the parking lot of the Knotty Pines restaurant. They'd made a date to meet, but when she pulled up and saw him in his shabby clothes, walking from his dented car toward the restaurant, she turned around and drove home.

When he called her an hour later, she said, "I guess I missed you."

A year later, my mother heard he'd been killed. He was drunk and got thrown from a horse, hit his head on a rock and cracked his skull open.

\*\*\*

My mother married Carl, and he moved into the Orange-wood apartment. She talked my grandmother into paying my rent for six months so she and Carl could be alone. I found a cute Spanish-style studio apartment, and Boris and I moved. He constantly ran away. I never knew if he'd come back. He took to stealing small objects: a sock, a letter, a pen, or pieces of kibble; hiding them under a chair, the bed, or the dining table; and crouching over them for hours at a time. He growled and bared his teeth if I tried to take them away. One day, while I was making hashish brownies, he jumped onto the kitchen counter and ate a gram of hash. He stumbled around for a couple hours and finally passed out. I worried it would kill him. I watched his breathing all day and night. The dog pound where Jack and I got him didn't say so, but I was sure he'd been abused.

After Kimberly "did her time" at St. Euphrasia, she came to Phoenix and moved in with my mother and Carl. They had a welcome home dinner for her. Carl cooked steaks for the four of us. "Poor kid probably hasn't had one the whole time she's been with those nuns," he said.

A welcome home party didn't make sense. My sister hadn't really come home. The last place she'd lived was Florida. She'd come back to a strange apartment and a step-father she'd never met.

When I saw her, she came toward me with her arms wide open. I expected our bodies to touch, but just before that might have happened, it seemed we both made a choice to keep a band of space between us.

"God is love," she said. She had a look, especially in her eyes—a God is love and no matter how shitty everything has been, hey, that's love too, veneer.

Kimberly stayed with my mother and Carl until she met Tiny and moved in with him. Tiny weighed 300 pounds and worked as a bouncer at the Pink Pony. I never met him. Kimberly said he was a friend helping her find a job and study for her GED. My mother was relieved when Kimberly left. She'd grown tired of hearing Bible quotes.

Nine months later, Kimberly had a baby girl, alone, at the county hospital in downtown Phoenix and gave it up for adoption. She hadn't told anyone she was pregnant. Why couldn't she have told me? Hadn't she known I would have helped her?

My mother thought she'd just gained weight, which she said was to be expected now that Kimberly was free and could eat anything she wanted. My sister didn't get very big so it didn't occur to me either that she might be pregnant; and she seemed to have taken the nun's teachings to heart, which must have included the evils of having sex outside of marriage. I tried but couldn't picture Kimberly having sex with 300-pound Tiny.

\*\*\*

One day, my sister came to see my new apartment. She sat with a towel over her shoulders, smoking a cigarette. She held a hand mirror and an ashtray in her lap while I cut her split ends and she told me about the baby.

"Are you all right?"

"Of course. It hurt like hell, but I'm a survivor. I couldn't have lived with myself if I'd had an abortion. She looked like Mother. I held her for a minute. It was weird holding a little Mother in my arms."

"Was it Tiny's?"

"No. Remember that cute guy Dave that worked at the gas station near Mother's apartment? He wanted to marry me, but I didn't love him. Don't cut too much."

"I'm not." I showed her a quarter inch of hair in the palm of my hand.

"She'll probably want to find me when she grows up. Don't you think?"

"I do." I wondered if there was a way to get her back now. I pictured my sister and me taking care of her. "Maybe when she's eighteen," I said.

"Don't tell Mother. Okay?" Kimberly held up the hand mirror and pulled pieces of her bangs over her eyes to check for evenness.

\*\*\*

"Why would she do such a thing?" my mother asked over lunch at the Sugar Bowl ice cream parlor.

"She looked like you," I said.

My mother's round blue eyes welled up; and for the first time, I felt a sense of justice.

"We could have figured something out," Mother said.

"Kimberly didn't think so." I took a bite of my ice cream.

My mother pushed her open-faced sandwich away, took a compact from her purse, and powdered her face. "Well, it's beyond me. After all I've done for her."

\*\*\*

Five years later, my sister called with the question, "Busy?" Her voice went up an octave on the y. I wanted to say, yes, I am busy, but I didn't. She said she'd decided to leave her husband and asked me to come for a visit. I'd accepted that using me as her sounding board whenever she had a problem had become the foundation of our relationship.

I flew from L.A., where I was now living, to Phoenix where Sky Harbor Airport had become complicated with sprawling terminals and multi-level parking structures. When Kimberly and I were small, gold and orange marigolds, planted in front of the only terminal, had spelled out the words "Welcome to Phoenix" visible only from the air.

I rented a car and drove to my sister's dirty stucco WWII house, purchased for her by my grandmother. She answered the door with a tennis ball in her right hand. I tried to hug her, and she backed away. "I can't hug you. My wrist and arm hurt. I've been trying to do the old exercises from rehab." I noticed yellowed sheets of notebook paper on the coffee table.

"From all those years ago?"

"I'm in training for a part-time job at 7-Eleven. Wally, the manager, says I'm great with the customers, but I need more speed on the register."

At twenty-one, Kimberly had suffered a stroke. The doctors said it was from birth control pills. She never finished physical therapy. She said the therapists were mean. Neither she nor my mother told me until I visited for Christmas almost a year later. When my mother finally spoke of it, she said, "What a mess. The wheelchair, the walker, and that rolling toilet. I couldn't stand to see her that way, a child of mine, a cripple. She couldn't talk or walk. It tore my guts out. They tied her tubes, said if she got pregnant again, it would kill her."

My sister's speech had come back, and unless she got nervous, she sounded like she used to. But her right wrist and hand were stiffened in the shape of a hook, and she dragged her right leg slightly behind her when she walked. When I first saw her, I wanted to scream. I thought I would burst open, break down, but I held it together until I was alone. Since then, no matter now much I rage or cry, there is no acceptance or consolation.

Now, we sat in soft armchairs. The foam had disintegrated, and there was too much sinking down. Kimberly crossed her still-thin legs and pumped the good, bare foot up and down, smoking in half time to the rhythm. A timer ticked in the kitchen.

"Do the imitation. Remember?"

She didn't skip a beat. She wound her good leg around the other at the knees and ankles, two twisted snakes. "Now girls," she said slurring the words, her wrist bent backwards, her cigarette lazily held between her fingers.

We laughed for a minute.

"I'm crossing my fingers for the job to work out," I said, showing her, but I couldn't imagine how she'd manage it.

"Me too. I'm cooking frozen potatoes for dinner."

"Frozen?"

"They have cheese on top. I didn't know what to make. I know you go out to nice restaurants. I figured anything frozen would be good enough."

"It's fine. So, what about Gregg?"

"He's too boring. I woke up one morning and realized I'd outgrown him. Mother said the same thing happened to her with all her husbands. I keep seeing myself dressed in a suit, carrying a briefcase, walking into one of those glass buildings in downtown Phoenix."

Gregg had been boring from the start. I hadn't liked him, but before I moved away, I tried to get along. He swaggered as he walked in his black cowboy boots, trying to be taller than he was, imagining himself a king in my sister's small two-bedroom house on Hubbell Street.

They'd just started dating when she had the stroke. He spoon-fed her and carried her back and forth to the bathroom. He worked nights as a security guard and drove a beer truck during the day. He handled everything.

"Gregg's taken good care of you." I hated being the voice of reason. She seemed to want to hear it, but then disregarded what I said with a snarling lip.

"I have a pen pal in Florence Prison. He's in for armed robbery and since I've been writing to him, he wants to get out and start a new life. I'd make a great counselor, don't you think?"

"I do, but you need some kind of training to do that."

"I asked you to come because I thought you could tell me what I should do next. Will you trim my bangs?"

The timer rang. I smelled burning cheese. My sister stood up, ground out the end of her filter tip, and picked up the ashtray, which she emptied after each cigarette. Her right leg dragged behind her as she headed for the kitchen.

# Abortos

One night in late summer of 1965, two months after we graduated from high school, Arlene and I drove three hours through the desert in ninety-five degree heat from Phoenix, where we lived, to Nogales, so she could get an abortion.

We'd been told to go to the bus depot on the American side and wait in the cafeteria for the doctor to approach us. When we walked in, pairs of brown eyes darted toward us—tired looking women in long skirts and men in faded black pants. Their children pointed and said, "*Mira, las gueras.*"

We sat at a long metal table on an attached bench, drank coffee, and smoked cigarettes. A huge clock, its face stained brownish yellow from food grease and dirt, hung on a paint-cracked wall. Its hands, barely visible, said 10:35. Our appointment was at eleven. An evaporative cooler rattled above our heads, spitting out hot, muggy air. I tried to conjure up a good outcome but couldn't help tensing the muscles in my chest and ribs, armoring myself for the possible butchering of Arlene that I would somehow have to handle. Raised Catholic, she feared God would punish us, and though we were almost in Mexico,

I worried that if God didn't get us, the U.S. government would. We were under age, but we could still be arrested and thrown in jail.

Arlene slumped in her seat, smoking with a shaky hand. We tried to look inconspicuous, which was impossible. All the people who came in and went out of the bus depot were dark-skinned, except for the two of us and a white man who sat a few feet away on the same bench. He wore a ponytail and a thin, spotty beard. His belly hung over a western-tooled belt that said "Jack Daniels" on the back. He half-smiled to no one as he held up a paper cup and picked his teeth with the straw that stuck up out of it.

I'd arranged everything, pretending I wanted the information for myself when I asked Donna, a divorced woman in my art class, what to do. Donna's drawings were confident and technically perfect and she was thirty-eight, so I trusted her. She wrote down a Mexican phone number, said to make the call from a phone booth, not to worry, it would be safe, she'd been through it herself.

"This must be him," I said, as a chubby man with glasses came through the front door and walked toward us. I flipped the lid of my Marlboro cigarette box, took out another cigarette, and lit it.

Arlene checked her watch. "It's not time yet."

I leaned over the table and whispered. "Well, he's coming this way. Don't look around." I dropped my head down and kept watching with lifted eyes. "Forget it. He turned."

Arlene wore a blue tank top. A gold Italian horn glistened at her throat. As usual, she had a dark tan and her short brown hair was bleached out from the sun. I wore blue too, a T-shirt that said *Fort Lauderdale*.

"I don't know why you said blue. This top is all I have and it's so tight since my boobs have grown."

"I told you. When I made the phone call, the woman asked what color we'd be wearing, so the doctor would know who we were. I was so nervous, I couldn't think. I scanned the inside of the phone booth and saw *Butterfield Blues Band* written on one of the metal slats with a heart drawn below it. You know how much I love them."

Arlene sighed and leaned across the table. "I could never have handled this alone."

"It's lucky I knew who to ask."

"I didn't tell Leonard or anyone but you. I have to end it with him. He's a drug dealer. Some of the people he hangs out with are scary. I'm so grateful you're here."

"Me too." I reached for her hand.

***

Arlene became my one and only friend the year I went to live with my grandmother. I didn't know anything about the old woman except that she drank too much and had money, but acted poor. Hanging out with Arlene helped make the situation bearable.

When I arrived, my grandmother told me if I obeyed her wishes, things might work out. She had two rules: no wasting electricity—"Like you're doing now," she'd said, "standing there with the refrigerator door open." And no lying.

But when I asked for something, it didn't matter what— gum, hairspray, a pair of jeans—her first response was, "I don't have the money," which I knew was a lie. Sometimes she'd give in, but only after I begged, which I wasn't very good at. All discussions had to happen in the morning.

She went to bed at four in the afternoon, after drinking straight shots of bourbon for three hours.

One day, on my way to Spanish class at my new school, where I hadn't made any friends, I walked by the fence that enclosed the football field. Dirty papers stuck like gray blinds in the diamond shaped holes. I passed the basketball courts where some guys were playing. The sun felt red-hot. I thought I might pass out. I held onto the fence and closed my eyes. A horn honked, and I jumped, startled to see a girl pulling up beside me in a red Corvette convertible. She screamed over the blasting radio, "Wanna go for a ride?"

"Sure," I said, looking over my shoulder to make sure she meant me.

"Hi, I'm Arlene." She turned down the radio. "I've seen you around."

"My name's Linda." I walked closer to the car.

"I know. We're in the same art history class."

"Oh, right."

"Get in."

I opened the door and slid into the red leather seat.

"You seem to know a lot about art. I've seen you sitting on the lawn drawing. What do you draw?" Arlene asked.

"Mostly nudes. I paint too. I signed up for a free life drawing class at the community college."

"That's cool. I'd like to see your stuff sometime. Hey, we could ditch school for the rest of the day. I know a great burger place we could go for lunch. The Ranch House. Ever been there?"

"No. Let's go."

Arlene was fearless behind the wheel. She drove seventy-five miles an hour on the winding highway that cut through Camelback Mountain where huge homes were scattered haphazardly like an updated version of Montezuma's castle.

"I used to try to draw horses, but I wasn't very good at it. I miss riding them." She drove with her right arm straight out, her knuckles turned white as she gripped the top of the leather-covered steering wheel. There was a rowdiness about her, which impressed and frightened me. "My father keeps promising to buy me a Palomino. They're so pretty." She said she'd been at Judson School for six months. She'd come from a big farm back in Ohio where all the horses had been sold. Her father had moved his construction business to Phoenix to make more money.

I lit a cigarette, twisted my bangs, and tried to think of things to say. Every once in a while, Arlene looked over and smiled at me. I could talk about art, but I'd never caught on to social friendliness. I knew there was a particular tone of voice and appropriate words to say, questions to ask, to get a positive reaction from another, but I couldn't bring myself to do it. Sometimes I felt like an extraterrestrial.

"Neat car," I said, finally.

"It is, right? But it's not mine. It's my boyfriend, Jerry's. You must have seen him around school. He only wears designer clothes, and he's destined to become a doctor. His parents own Montoya's, a chain of Mexican restaurants in Arizona and Nevada."

"Cool," I said, pretending to be impressed. Jerry was in my Spanish class. I hadn't talked to him, but I could tell he was a snob. He walked with a swagger in tight pants and lizard skin Italian shoes. I'd heard him bragging about the leather to a group of boys. He wore a diamond and gold pinky ring, and he twisted and flashed it like he was in the Mafia.

Arlene pulled up in front of the Ranch House, a small wooden building next door to a gas station. Two old ladies, originally from Bisbee, did the cooking with nets over their hair.

Out back, at a picnic table, Arlene dumped her fries out onto a napkin. "So, do you have a boyfriend?"

"Back in Florida. He's much older, a lifeguard at the beach. He models too. Cigarette ads for magazines."

"Wow."

"John treated my foot one day at the beach when a stingray stung me so badly I could hardly walk. We dated that summer until I came here."

"Have you gone all the way?"

I'd been afraid to, but I didn't want Arlene to know that. I took a bite of my cheeseburger and didn't answer.

"Jerry and I do it all the time. Some days I can hardly walk I'm so sore after a night with him. Know what I mean?"

I pushed some fries into my mouth and swallowed hard. "I know what you mean." I wondered if Arlene made the same strange moaning sounds I'd heard from my mother.

"Want to come to my house on Saturday? We could bleach our hair."

I must have said the right things. "Sounds great."

"I could fix you up sometime with one of Jerry's friends. We could double date."

"Maybe," I said, knowing I wouldn't like his friends and wondering when I'd go all the way.

\*\*\*

Arlene's family included me in holiday and Sunday dinners. For Christmas, I gave each of them their portraits painted in acrylic and oil. Her mother took me to my first gynecological appointment. Her father took us out to lunch in celebration of our birthdays and Arlene's saint's day. And when my paintings were shown at Baboquivari's, the local coffee house, Arlene came to the opening with her parents and two brothers. It was too late in the day for my grandmother to come. Spending time with Arlene's family reminded me of what I believed I'd had with Jack, and what I'd lost.

Arlene and I spent all our time together except when she was with Jerry. We cruised Central Avenue and practiced smoking. Like my mother and most girls I'd seen, Arlene's boyfriend came first. I had to accept it or be friendless. I couldn't find a boyfriend I liked. I kept things going with John, writing letters back and forth. He sent me gifts, mostly Tiki god necklaces. One had real rubies for eyes. Arlene wanted to wear that one.

I accepted a blind date once, a friend of Jerry's. But when he came to the door, I couldn't bring myself to open it. I'd put on make-up and my best sweater. My hands shook, my ankles wobbled in high heels. I looked through the door's peephole. Except for his blond hair, the guy looked like Jerry's twin. I talked through the intercom. "I'm sick," I said. "I can't go out." I told Arlene I was too much in love with John to date other people.

We graduated from high school, and my grandmother bought me a used car with a column shifter and no radio. Arlene's father took up with a young woman named Trudy, and the whole family fell apart. I felt the same as I had every time my mother divorced. My spine seemed to shrink. My back and neck ached from the pressure, but no one could tell by looking at me. I'd gotten good at swallowing all kinds of fears, including ones I couldn't name. I'd learned to be brave.

Charles and Trudy left town and never came back. That's when Arlene got a job as a topless go-go dancer at the Tradewinds Bar in downtown Phoenix.

She'd been afraid to go alone, so I went with her to the audition.

"Your tits ain't big enough," the manager said to me, thinking I was there to audition too. He was fat and sweaty. He fingered a small cross that hung from a tight gold chain around his neck.

I crossed my arms over my chest and stepped away. "Not me," I said.

Every night, for the first few weeks, I sat at a round Formica table and watched Arlene dance. Colored lights flashed from the ceiling. She rubbed her hands over her breasts and rotated her hips. She moved her arms like waves through the air. She shook her whole body up and down, side to side. Her feet spun her in circles across the floor. Men in faded jeans and dusty cowboy boots made loud whooping noises. I felt embarrassed for Arlene, but at least she didn't smile at them.

On her break, she'd join me at the table. We'd talk until she had to dance again, and I'd go home to my grand-mother.

"This is so weird," she'd say. "These guys are such creeps."

But when I asked her if she was sure about this, she said, "I make good money," in a flat voice with a stony face. Having been her father's princess, daddy's girl, I knew that more than anything, she was doing this to crush him and to get back at Jerry, who had dumped her when her family fell apart.

When men approached our table and said things like, "Hey sweetheart, that's some fine dancin'," I'd clench my teeth and glare at them. "If you don't mind, we're having a private conversation."

"Just tryin' to be friendly."

One night, I came late and saw Arlene standing at the bar in the short nylon robe she wore at break time. She was laughing, surrounded by men. One of them had his arm around her waist. One guy yelled, "Hey, Linda. How ya doin' babe?" Arlene waved for me to join them.

How did they know my name? What was Arlene doing?

"Come on over," she said. "These guys are okay."

I couldn't move.

One of them said, "We were tellin' Arlene what a fine dancer she is. How about showin' us what you can do." He wiggled his hips, and they all laughed.

I stood there staring in disbelief, choking back my disgust.

"Oh, well," the guy said.

"Forget her," said another.

They all turned away from me and huddled around Arlene. I walked out and never went back.

We didn't call each other after that. I tried to paint but couldn't concentrate. There was a gnawing in my stomach. The odor of oil paint and turpentine made my eyes sting. I'd end up staring, glassy-eyed at the muddy canvas, smoking cigarettes and sucking on frozen chocolate turtles.

One day, I sat at the kitchen table trying to eat a sandwich. My grandmother sat across from me snapping cards down for solitaire and asked me when I'd be getting a job. "That's why I bought you the car. Weren't you and Arlene going to get a place together?"

"I'm not sure," I said.

"Maybe you should go back to your mother."

"You know I can't. It might still work out with Arlene. I'm going to call her right now."

She said she was living with a guy named Leonard. "He's a bartender at the Safari Hotel. We have a good thing going. I'm meeting all kinds of interesting people. You probably wouldn't like them."

"Oh, I might," I lied.

"What have you been up to?"

"Working on some paintings. I'm thinking about applying to art school. Maybe we could get together."

"Sure, I'll call you."

I didn't expect to hear from her, but soon after that she called. She was in trouble and didn't know who else she could trust. She made me promise not to tell anyone. At first, I didn't know exactly what to do, but I knew I'd think of something. I had to. Arlene and I had been best friends for two years and if everything worked out, maybe we could be close again. Maybe we'd get a place together and she'd go back to the way she was before.

\*\*\*

Waiting with her in the bus depot in Nogales, I thought of the times during high school we spent Saturdays getting stoned and changing the color of each other's hair. "Remember when we dyed my hair auburn?"

"That was the best color on you. Much better than when it turned green."

"Oh, I'd forgotten about the green." I put my head down and laughed.

Suddenly, a slender, Mexican man, about forty, was standing next to Arlene. He wore a polyester short-sleeve shirt with a tie and gray pants. His hair was combed down with something shiny. He smelled like lemons.

"You waiting for me?" He swung his legs over the bench and sat down next to Arlene. She leaned away from him.

"You have the envelope?"

The woman on the phone had said 200 dollars in small bills, sealed in a white envelope.

Arlene handed it to him under the table.

His nails looked clean, and he wore a nice watch and a wedding ring. I told myself this was a good sign.

"I go out now, and you follow," he said. "In the parking lot, I have a brown Chevy. You drive behind me in your car. What kind do you have?"

"A '61 white Plymouth."

"Across the border, three miles, is a hotel, two stories. There is no name. Look for a flashing sign that says *Bar*. You get a room. I watch from the parking lot. After you're in, I come to the door. Okay?"

I nodded in agreement, and he left. I picked up my lighter and box of cigarettes, put them in my purse. I tried to remember everything he'd said.

"Let's go," I said. I untangled my legs from under the table, lifted them over the bench, and stood up. Arlene didn't move. "Arlene, we should go now."

"What do you think?"

I put my hand on her shoulder. "I think he's okay. We should go."

Outside, the night was hotter than before, the air crackling with dryness. There were no streetlights and the moon was too thin to light our way.

"I think that's him," said Arlene. "Over there." She pointed to a pair of uneven headlights off to the right. "What if he drives away with the money?"

I hadn't thought of that. "He won't."

I tugged at Arlene's arm, and we walked faster toward

my car. We climbed in, and I started it up, followed him across the border through the blackened desert into Mexico. The highway disappeared behind us. Ahead, we barely saw the flickering *Bar* sign. It looked like a dying signal from a space ship that had landed long ago, still trying to get a response from Earth.

We got a room on the second floor facing the gravel parking lot. The room was small and dark. The curtains and bedspread were a purple and black print, made from cheap rough cotton. It looked clean enough. I parted the curtains and peeked out.

He got out of his car with a doctor's bag. Donna had said he was a real doctor. I thought about what kinds of instruments were in that bag and wondered how often he did this. My chest felt tight. I closed the crack in the curtain and heard his small feet crunch on the gravel.

Arlene sat on the bed with tears in her eyes. "You know I tried to get a blessing from Father Michael. He wouldn't give it. He said it's been too long since I've been to church."

I sat down next to her. I wasn't Catholic, and I couldn't imagine a blessing from a priest making any kind of difference.

The doctor tapped on the door, and I let him in. He put down his bag and shook both our hands. "I am Doctor Medellin." He didn't ask our names, and we didn't give them. "Which one?" he asked. I nodded toward Arlene. "Nothing to worry. How far along?"

"*Más o menos siete o ocho semanas,*" Arlene said. We'd figured out how to say this from what we learned in high school Spanish class.

He opened his bag and pulled out a needle and vial of something. "You leave," he said to me. "Come back in two hours."

"I didn't think I'd have to leave."

"Neither did I," said Arlene.

"I think it'll be okay. What is that, anyway?" I asked the doctor.

"To make her sleep. She will not feel a thing. I cannot start if you are here."

"I'll leave after you give her the shot."

He gave Arlene the injection, and I stood up to leave. "I'll be back soon, Arlene. Don't worry."

"I feel fine. Just fine." She was already getting groggy.

I didn't want to abandon her, but I didn't know what else to do. I got in my car and rolled the windows down part way, locked the doors, and sat there staring up at Room 235. Now that I was alone, I wanted to cry about what was happening, but I had to stay alert in so much darkness in the middle of nowhere. My body began to sweat, struggling with the heat and fear. Crickets chirped off in the distance. I'd read somewhere they were a sign of good luck. I took a deep breath and looked at myself in the rear view mirror. *Smart*, I thought. I'd handled everything. My grandmother thought I was in Tucson on job interviews, staying overnight with Jane, a girl from Judson who'd called and wanted to get together. I knew she and her family were on vacation. I gave my grandmother a made up phone number, knowing she'd never call. There was no way she could find out about this trip unless something happened to Arlene.

But it wouldn't. Soon everything would be back to normal. I would get a job, maybe something to do with art. And I'd move in with Arlene.

I kept track of time. I'd been in the car for forty-five minutes when a pair of headlights shined in the mirror and I heard tires grind through the dry air. A car pulled up behind me. A man emerged and walked toward me weaving back and forth. He had long hair and a moustache.

"Where is she?" he said into my half-open window. His speech was slurred.

My heart pounded through my veins. My fingers shook as I felt for the handle, rolled up the window as fast as I could.

"I know she's here."

"I have no idea what you're talking about," I yelled through the glass. I realized this had to be Leonard, and he must have followed us. I didn't know what he might do.

"Where is she?" He started toward the hotel, his arms swinging around his tight, muscled body. I had to keep him away from Arlene. I got out of the car and ran in his direction.

"I've got a gun," he said.

More courage arose and snapped me out of my body. I planted myself directly in front of him, put my hands on my hips. "What are you going to do, shoot her?"

"I don't know," he said in a quieter voice. He looked down, his arms went limp. The gun swung from his finger like a toy.

"Let's get in the car," I said. I led him away from the hotel. "Put the gun away." He slipped it under the seat. I pulled slowly out of the parking lot and drove up and down the streets of Nogales making sure I kept the *Bar* sign in view. We drove in silence.

I slid my eyes to the side and glared at him. He smelled like stale beer. Arlene must have met him at the Tradewinds Bar. Snobby Jerry was a prize in comparison.

"I know what she's doing down here," he said.

"I don't think so."

"She told me about having to wear a certain color and all that. Pretty far out."

"What?" I stopped the car.

"I didn't believe it was mine at first, but you know I've been thinking about this one night we made love where it felt like something was there that was never there before. Know what I mean? Of course, that doesn't mean I want to keep it."

I leaned my arms and then my head on the steering wheel.

"You okay?"

"Shut up," I said, my voice like a growl.

"What's with you?"

I jerked the car into gear and drove back to the hotel. "Get out."

"Hey, I don't know what your problem is. I don't even know you ..."

"Get out."

"Okay, okay. Tell Arlene I'll be in the bar. She'd better be all right."

Leonard retrieved his gun and got out of the car. He lumbered across the parking lot, dragging his shoes through the gravel.

"Bastard." I rubbed my scalp. My head felt like thousands of pins pricking the inside of my skull. I held my forehead with my right hand and got out of the car.

The doctor's car was still in the parking lot, but the two hours were up. I wanted to talk to Arlene, hear her explanation.

I knocked at room 235. The doctor opened it and stood there wiping his hands carefully on a towel. The room smelled of sweet lemon cologne.

"Just finished," he said.

"Is she all right?" I moved closer to Arlene, passed out on the bed, covered with a blanket. She was still breathing.

"Everything's fine. A little bleeding for a few days. Nothing to worry. Do you want to see it?" His eyes got bigger, and he smiled.

"See it?"

"It's in the toilet."

"God, no."

He went to the bathroom and flushed. He came back, still smiling and rubbing his hands together. He sat down on one of the chairs. "What's your name?"

I looked over at Arlene and said nothing.

He crossed his legs and leaned back in the chair. "She will be out until the morning. I order some drinks from the bar. What do you like?"

"You'd better go."

"We have a party, no?"

My hands began to sweat. He wasn't going to budge. I cleared my throat and crossed my arms over my stomach. He could do whatever he wanted and no one would know. Who could I call for help in Mexico? Leonard was it. I watched myself pick up the phone and ask for the bar.

The doctor said, "I like scotch."

I put my hand over the mouthpiece and said, "I'm calling her boyfriend to come up. He's been waiting downstairs. He has a gun. If I were you, I'd get out of here as fast as I could." The bar answered, and I asked for Leonard. "Come up to room 235."

The doctor grabbed his bag, ran out the door.

"Creep," I said to his back. I watched from the window as he slipped on the gravel and headed toward his car. Arlene looked peaceful and innocent. I was furious. My chest and throat tingled with heat. The doctor's wheels spun as he took off through the parking lot.

For the rest of the night, I sat draped over a chair, clutching a pillow and chain smoking, waiting for the double-crossing Arlene to wake up. Leonard dozed in the other chair, holding the gun in his lap. I wanted to pull the trigger right where the barrel was aimed. I hated that he'd become my rescuer. But at least he didn't know that.

Before daylight, Arlene began to stir. I woke Leonard and told him to go get coffee. I wanted Arlene alone. I sat on the edge of the chair and watched her wake up. Her face was soft and puffy, mascara globbed under her eyes.

"How do you feel?"

"Fine, I think." Arlene pulled back the blanket and sat up. "But I'm pretty sure that guy had sex with me right before I passed out. I could have dreamed it."

I didn't care. "Leonard's here."

"Where?"

"He knew everything."

"Where is he?"

"You said I was the only one who knew."

"I couldn't help but tell him."

"Why did you lie?"

"I didn't think you'd help me."

"Of course I would."

"Look, he followed me here. That proves he loves me."

Arlene got up and moved slowly to the bathroom. Over running water she said, "You know Linda, your problem is you've always been jealous of my boyfriends."

I felt the acid in my stomach rise up into my throat and mouth. The sour taste was sickening. It was all I could do to gulp it down. I could have strangled her.

"How can you say that?" I shouted into the bathroom.

"I don't have the energy to discuss this now. I'll drive home with Leonard. I'll call you later. Thanks for everything."

Leonard came back to the room and they left. I stood by the window, barely breathing. My chest felt like a cave. I watched him help her navigate the stairs. They got in his car, then sped off down the highway.

When they were out of sight, I made my way to the parking lot. The sun climbed up the sky as I made the long drive home. I'd worried about Arlene being butchered, but now I felt permanently cracked open. What would I tell my grandmother about the job interviews?

***

I got home to find all my clothes and belongings in a pile in the driveway. My whole body went numb. I couldn't believe my grandmother wanted me out of the house so badly she would resort to this. She must have gone on a binge. I rang the doorbell over and over. I banged on the door, screamed, "Grandma, why did you do this? Let me in."

After several minutes, the old woman came to the door, drunk, wearing only a pajama top. She weaved back and forth behind the locked screen. "You lied to me."

"I did not."

"That Jane called here, tried to cover for you, but you can't fool me, missy."

"Okay, okay," I said, half choking, still trying to swallow my failure. "I had to help Arlene. She needed an abortion. She made me promise not to tell anyone. I was trying to be a good friend. What's so bad about that?"

My grandmother didn't say a word. Her eyes closed. She held onto the doorframe. She looked like she might pass out. Finally, she unlocked the screen door and wobbled down the hall to her bedroom. "Don't forget to turn on the burglar alarm."

I dragged my things back into the house, making as much noise as possible.

# Art Lessons

The summer I turned sixteen, my mother moved back to Phoenix. My grandmother rented her an apartment on the condition that I move in with her. I didn't want to but my grandmother was more than ready for me to leave her house. When I showed my mother the art I'd been doing and told her I wanted to go to art school, she didn't pay much attention, but a couple weeks later she said she knew a local professional artist who she thought held classes in his studio. "Maybe your grandmother will pay for it." I wondered if she wanted to help me because she hadn't been around for so many years. Maybe she thought I had talent. She'd told me that when I was a baby, I pointed at a print of Van Gogh's "Sunflowers" hanging on the wall and said my first word, "pretty."

She took me to Paul Roberge's studio. He told her he didn't accept everyone and that I had to bring samples of my work. He was the best artist in Phoenix, known for his drawing and painting skills and his many public sculptures and murals including the "Phoenix Bird" at Sky Harbor Airport. My mother thought the "Phoenix Bird" was "God-awful," but most everyone else saw it as a beautiful rendition of the symbol of the city. I liked its semi-abstractness, bright colors, and that Paul had used natural materials from the Hopi and Navajo reservations in its construction.

My mother said she remembered him from years ago when she used to model. He'd come to the Wigwam Resort and the Westward Ho on modeling days and sketch her and the other models as they walked the make-shift runway by the swimming pool while guests ate lunch under striped umbrellas. Sometimes I modeled with my mother in a matching child's version of her outfit. We'd hold hands, pose, then pivot at the end of the runway, the skirts of our dresses lifting and twirling like fans opening into the hot desert air. But I didn't remember Paul.

She said when she performed at the Sombrero Play-house in *Lady in the Dark*, he came back stage one night wearing a black cape. "He was very dramatic. He kissed my hand and asked me to pose for him, which I never did. I wore a chignon in those days. He must be in his sixties now. He's French, and he has a thing about Indians."

Paul's studio was attached to a small three-bedroom adobe house, adjacent to the Indian School Road canal, encircled by paloverde and eucalyptus trees and twelve-foot-high white and pink oleander bushes.

He'd just finished lunch and was wiping his teeth with a cloth napkin when we arrived. He was tall with gray-white hair. A square patch of moustache sat perfectly under-neath his nose. His steel blue eyes were both inviting and penetrating as if he could see things about me that I didn't see. His chiseled face tilted upward and moved slightly from side to side as if he were bothered by smells in the air. He wore sienna-colored moccasins, which wrapped around the outside of his ankles, held together with silver buttons. A turquoise bolo tie in the shape of a Zuni sun hung from his neck.

Kachina dolls and miniature French flags and soldiers sat on shelves above the desk in his office. He told us he'd recently been named the French consul of Arizona. He was a good friend of Helen Luce and Marcel Marceau, and his mother had been a Russian princess. He'd grown up in France, started the Boy Scouts in Paris, and moved to Arizona to study the Navajo and Hopi Indians. He was an honorary member of the Hopi tribe.

"Remember me?" my mother said. "From the Wigwam?"

"Of course," he said, but I could tell he didn't. My mother knew it too. She fluffed her hair and cleared her throat. "I'll wait here," she said, sitting on the couch in the den.

Paul took me to the studio. It smelled of turpentine, oil paint, and charcoal. Work tables were piled high with stacks of drawing pads, sketches of naked woman, all kinds of pens and pencils, different sized broad knives, a palate, and huge jars of paint. Blank canvases were stacked up in a corner. Paintings of women with very long hair leaned against the walls—one with braids that curved down and up around her breasts; another with hair tangled in a man's hands; one of an American Indian woman who wore smooth, thick, spiraling buns on each side of her head. Others had hair flowing down in sheets of black, reddish blonde, or brown. All were realistically portrayed in glistening oil paint. I wanted to pick up the brushes I saw sitting upside down in red coffee cans, like magician's wands, and be able to paint like that.

I showed him my tree drawings, the collages I'd made in art classes at school, and my best painting, a copy of Goya's "Saturn Devouring One Of His Sons," which looked more like his daughter in my version. The coolness of the cement studio floor eased through my thin leather-soled thongs.

"Ah. Very honest," he said. I didn't know what he meant, but I hoped it was enough for him to accept me as a student.

He asked me to write a visual description of anything I liked and to come back in two weeks. Paul kissed my mother's right hand, then mine. He said something in French as he unlatched the heavy wooden double doors of the studio. My mother's red polished toenails lost what was left of their shine as we walked through the dirt driveway to the car.

\*\*\*

By the time I went back to see Paul, I'd had my shoulder-length hair cut short in a geometric style and I'd started working part-time as a shoeshine girl at the Safari Hotel barbershop. Jiggs, the owner, told me to wear hot pants and smile a lot. Sometimes I had to clean and polish six pairs of cowboy boots covered with horseshit, but the tips were good. My mother had heard about the job from the bartender at the Safari and encouraged me to apply.

"What a fun way to make money!" she'd said. "And you're the very first shoeshine girl in all of Arizona." My mother was a natural flirt, and I was not. I think she thought the job would be a good way to earn money and give me the flirtation training I needed. I hated bending over men's shoes with a mirror behind me, but I learned that the more I smiled and the shorter my shorts, the more money I made.

Paul read my paper: a description of a mother and her two children playing and laughing together on a beach.

He said I veered off the visual into a description of feelings, but he could tell I had an artistic sensibility. Even with the barbershop job, I couldn't afford the twenty-five dollars an hour he charged for lessons. He offered to trade private and group classes for studio work. My duties would include bookkeeping, cleaning the studio, washing his brushes, stretching canvas, running errands, setting up easels and supplies for his art classes, and occasional portrait modeling. He'd provide a meal on the days I worked.

He was upset I'd cut my hair so short because it would be more difficult to attach hairpieces when I modeled.

"A woman is made for long hair," he said. "Below the hips, below her sex. American women cut off sexuality."

"Short hair is much easier to take care of," I said.

"Ah, but with long hair, a woman becomes different each day. She can wear her hair up or down, in braids. It is endless, and the man stays interested."

"What does the man do to keep the woman interested?"

"The nature of woman is to love one man and focus attention on him. The nature of man is to love many women."

That didn't sound right to me. But he must know. He was French.

Paul said the job was mine if I'd let my hair grow. I agreed to the trade and had my first art lesson.

He covered a wooden stool with a piece of black velvet, carefully set an egg on top, then angled two overhead flood lights to create shadows. He handed me a newsprint pad and a stick of charcoal.

"Be sure to include everything you see. I'll be back in a while."

"Can I have some music?" I asked.

"No."

I stared at the egg and thought he must be kidding. I wanted to use big brushes, spread thick color on canvas. I lit a cigarette and drew the outline of the egg. Slowly, I began to see shapes of light and shadow. I made small marks inside the outline and smudged them into little patches of gray, some blacker than others. My drawing looked like an oval patchwork quilt, not an egg.

Paul came back in an hour and handed me a glass of wine. "Good. Now, train yourself to see patterns of variegated light and shadow in everything."

The next night, I set up the studio and attended his life drawing class. He had six students: two retired army men, three tan housewives from the neighborhood who were very enamored with Paul, and me. We did quick sketches of the first nude model I'd ever seen. I was surprised she didn't seem embarrassed. She changed poses when a timer went off: every minute, then every three minutes, then five.

"Why are we drawing so fast?" I asked Paul.

"Hesitation breeds bad art. The eye sees, the mind sketches, the hand only obeys. It is important to observe all the time, sketch all the time, wherever you go."

The model's eyes never looked at any of us directly. When she took a break, she went outside in her little blue robe and smoked. Her hair hung down to her knees. Paul told her to pin it up for the quick sketches and then release it for the longer pose we drew at the end of the evening.

I spent three nights a week and Sundays at the studio. When I arrived, Paul would smile and say, "*Ya te he.*" A Hopi greeting. I stayed late in the evenings to wash his brushes with turpentine and Castille soap. On Sunday mornings, before we went to work, I made instant coffee the way he liked it, in a big ceramic mug with four teaspoons of sugar and thick cream. Instant coffee didn't seem very French to me.

To round up students and try to sell his art, Paul did a portrait painting demonstration once a month for groups like the Kiwanis Club, the Chamber of Commerce, and circles of women in private homes who'd studied art in college and were now docents at the Heard Museum. They'd hover around Paul before and after the demonstration, each vying for his attention with wine, cheese, cookies, and practiced questions about art. I set up his easel, brushes, and tubes of paint and sat for the portrait. I wore a long hairpiece that hung down the middle of my back. I attached it onto my own pulled-back hair and covered the line of demarcation with a black headband. Paul was impressed with how still I could be. I liked seeing my face emerge into a painting. He made me look older than I was.

When Señor Tico's, a new Mexican restaurant in Scottsdale, commissioned Paul to design a marketplace mural, I helped him paint pink and red flowers with green vines and leaves around the arched doorways. I was afraid of making a mistake, but he gave me a pattern to follow and said he had confidence in me.

I did life drawings of fruit, flowers, Kachina dolls, and nude women. My skills improved. I made a color wheel with corresponding tones of white, gray, and black. I did a painting exercise in the dark to learn about light. I couldn't stop looking at my first self-portrait. It was realistic and abstract. The paint was thick, the brushstrokes a mixture of bold and refined. It was an image I'd never seen in the mirror, only felt deep in my stomach. I'd painted my insides, made visible a gnawing crookedness I had no words for. Paul said making art was like an archeological dig.

He put on an art show with his student's work, and I sold three drawings.

He took me to the Hopi reservation for the snake dances. He said I needed to experience something other than my white American culture, that exposure to Hopi life would be good for my development as an artist.

"You can sketch, but no photographs, and you have to wear a skirt on the reservation or they will think you are a hippie. The Hopi don't like hippies, especially the ones that show up half naked to watch their ceremonies."

We drove Paul's old Chevrolet station wagon up the mountain road to Second Mesa. He'd been going there since the 1940s, before there was a road that went all the way to the top. He'd ridden a mule in those days. He told me the Hopi had dances for every occasion, even one to instruct children in sex.

I wished I'd had some instruction, I thought.

"White people are not allowed to see that one," he said.

When we arrived at Second Mesa, Paul got out of the car and said, "*Ya te he!*" as he handed out gifts of chicken and coffee to the Hopi women who greeted us.

Paul showed me around the reservation before the dances started. I noticed some large snow white feathers on the ground and I bent down to pick one up.

"What kind of bird do these come from?"

He grabbed my shoulder and said, "Don't touch it."

"Why not?"

"It's part of a sacred prayer ceremony. You have to be more respectful. White people think everything belongs to them." He sprinkled some cornmeal from a little reddish brown pouch that hung from his belt, around the feather I'd almost touched. Then he sprinkled me.

"Let's go," Paul said. "It is time."

We sat on hard folding chairs in the plaza. The Mud-Head Kachinas, the clowns called Koyemsi, were dressed exactly like the Kachina dolls in Paul's den. Their bodies were painted in brown mud. They wore black skirts and headpieces made of mud with holes for their eyes and mouth. I got out my sketchbook and began to draw.

Other Hopi men, dressed as Snake people, appeared wearing loincloths and feathers. They carried gourds and seashell rattles. The crowd became quiet. The snake men began to move in a circle around the plaza in a repetitious stepping dance choreographed to the sound of their rattles. The monotone rhythm created a trance state. My body seemed to dissolve into the sound. For a moment, I slipped out of my mind. My usual thoughts seemed to un-stick themselves from my brain. I began to sketch abstract shapes I'd never seen or imagined. When I looked up, the men were extracting snakes from a bush, putting them in their mouths, between their teeth as they continued stepping.

"Rattlesnakes," Paul said.

"Does anyone ever die?" I whispered.

"Never."

Paul's eyelids began to flutter. His body made tiny spiraling movements. I'd seen him do this sometimes when he was painting.

After a while, the men put the snakes gently on the ground, and soon the plaza was full of slithering reptiles. A man with a stick poked at the snakes until they were in a pile. Finally, the dancing men grabbed them and carried them out to the desert in four directions, to the west, south, east, and north. The plaza became quiet.

Being on top of the mesa, I could look out as far as I could see. A quiet breeze carried smoke and herb smells from the Kiva. A gust of wind blew my skirt up. I pulled it tight over my knees and held it down. This was the first time I'd felt like a minority. The Hopi lived a tribal life, protected by some kind of ancient reality. I wanted to be one of them.

Paul came out of his trance. "Now, rain will come," he said.

And the next day, rain did come. It poured down as I worked on a painting of the snake dance trying to recapture how I'd felt on the reservation. In the afternoon, a model that was scheduled to pose that night for Paul's new painting got sick and cancelled. He asked me to fill in. I'd have to pose nude, and it would be extra money. Fifteen dollars an hour. He made a Brie cheese omelet for dinner. Whipping the eggs he said, "I do not understand you Americans keeping butter and cheese in the refrigerator. Cheese is alive!"

After dinner, he handed me a robe. I took off my clothes in the bathroom, looked in the mirror, experimented with the confident and nonchalant expressions I'd seen on the models I'd drawn in class. I sucked in my stomach, put on the robe, and walked to the studio. Paul attached long, stiff hairpieces to my head, then laid out fake tree branches, pieces of driftwood, small twigs, and an antler horn on a hard, wooden platform covered with shiny red and purple fabric.

"I'll be right back," I said. I went to the kitchen and downed a few gulps of Russian vodka from the bottle. I went back to the studio, quickly threw off the robe, and lay down. Paul wound my fake hair around the branches and the antler. He turned on floodlights. Heat beat down on my skin from every corner of the platform. He climbed up and down a ladder, hovered over me, taking photographs from different angles. Then he made insistent scratching sounds on paper, sketching me in different poses, occasionally rearranging the hair.

I started to feel aroused. The vodka had helped me relax. The theme from *Doctor Zhivago* played in the background. I was sure Paul would seduce me, and I wanted him to. The more he looked at me, the more sensual I felt. I wondered if he'd lean over and kiss me or lie down next to me. Would he carry me to his bed? If we had sex, I imagined I could ingest everything he knew about art.

"Ah. You are beautiful," he said. "You are very beautiful. You were made for the south of France. Look up. Look up. A little to the right. There, that curve there. That's it. Now you are in the perfect light. The sensuous mouth. Lovely. Have you ever made love to an older man?"

"Yes."

"How old was he?"

"Twenty-six."

"Was he an artist?"

"A dancer. In Florida he's known as the Limbo King."

\*\*\*

Lennie was the first man I had sex with. We met in Fort Lauderdale when I was fourteen. He was twenty-six. He had a Beatle haircut and at six-foot-four, lean and long-limbed, he could wiggle his way under a limbo pole seven inches from the ground.

One night when my mother went out, I gave my virginity to the Beatle-haired limbo king. I wore a vintage

1940s see-through black lace nightgown for the occasion, sprayed my arms and neck with my mother's Chanel No. 5 perfume. The insistence in his hands startled me. He began to kiss me everywhere. He smelled like Coppertone and salt water.

"I've wanted to fuck you since the first time I saw you," he said.

"I haven't gone all the way before."

"Yeah, right." He thought I was eighteen.

He led me to the bedroom, where I'd lit five peach-scented candles. His hands slid under the nightgown, rubbing my legs, stomach, breasts, and inner thighs. He tried to enter me and couldn't. He kept trying and finally spread me open. I moaned with pain. He made panting noises and said "Oh, baby," over and over again.

Afterwards, fluids seeped out of me. I knew some of it was blood. I didn't show Lennie the proof. I ran to the bathroom to avoid staining my mother's sheets.

When she suspected I'd had sex, she said, "I hope you're not sleeping with him because if you are, he won't respect you."

*Who's respecting you?* I thought.

Sometimes, when I came home from a date, I'd see a guy sneaking out of the apartment, shoes in his hand, a jacket draped over his arm. I'd wait until he walked down the street to his car, then go inside in pitch-blackness as my mother pretended to be asleep. I didn't tell her I saw these men. She couldn't take being called a hypocrite. So I let her think she was fooling me.

Lying amidst branches and twigs, I wondered what sex would be like with Paul. What French things would he do?

"Mmm. The hair looks natural on you. It is sexy."

I turned my head to face him. "Will this be a painting of me with my face and body, or are you just using me to get the right proportions?"

"Please do not move."

"Did you look at the self-portrait I did last week?"

"Very original. Honesty is the basis of true art. And remember, an artist is creative. Stay original. Never be a robot or a sheep. Have a contrary mind to be original, but do not become so much so as to veer on the sensational, like our friend Picasso."

Paul said this with an envious tone. I could tell he wanted to get into a debate so he could make his case against Picasso, but I already knew what competition felt and sounded like. "So I definitely have talent?" I said.

"Most definitely. All great artists have been, at first, amateurs."

"Were you ever married?"

"A long time ago. I have a daughter."

"Did your wife have long hair?"

"Of course. I would not be attracted to a woman who didn't."

"Do you have a girlfriend?"

"I have many. Perhaps I have a new one."

He stopped sketching. I felt my body flush. I closed my eyes, ready for his touch. But he didn't make his move. He started sketching again. "I met a half-Hopi, half-Italian woman I want to paint."

I thought he'd meant that I could be his new girlfriend. My body felt like dead weight as I posed for another hour in a different position.

"Voilà," he finally said and sent me home after I cleaned up the studio.

I didn't tell my mother about the nude modeling.

She wouldn't have tried to stop me, but I thought she might be jealous. She got that way when she didn't have a boyfriend. We'd go out to dinner, and she'd ooze sexuality with the busboys, waiters, any man in the place. I still cared about her feelings then, so I'd make a half-hearted effort to compete, felt guilty if I didn't. And she'd always be the winner.

I did more nude modeling for Paul, but he never made a move. My artwork continued to improve, began to look professional. The kind of abstract images I'd sketched on the reservation began to appear in my work—shapes of color faintly resembling human figures seemed to paint themselves onto my canvases. But I was also preoccupied thinking about sex with Paul, why he wasn't interested after seeing me naked in all kinds of sensual poses. He started taking me to the Chris-Town shopping mall to look for young women with long hair. When he spotted one, he'd send me over to do the talking.

"Ask if they would like to model for a professional artist. Ask for their name and phone number and give them my card."

I didn't want anyone else to pose for him, so I lied and told him none of the women were interested. I started wearing my hairpiece every day after that.

I guess my mother could tell I was falling in love with Paul. Maybe she read my journal or found the nude drawings I'd done of him. One day she told me she'd read an article in *Vogue* magazine that said young girls had a tendency to think they were in love with older men, particularly if they didn't have a father. She stood up, cleared her throat, and re-arranged the turquoise and silver bangle bracelets on her arm. She left the room and never mentioned it again.

\*\*\*

I worked for Paul off and on for the next three years. After that first summer and as I got older, my longing for him faded. When I was twenty, in town visiting my newly married mother, I saw Paul one day in the studio. His vision had become spotty, and I helped him finish a commissioned portrait. He said I knew his style better than anyone. After the day's work, we talked and drank vodka into the night. He kissed me, and we ended up in bed. I didn't know if it was the alcohol or his age or both, but he couldn't get it up. His penis was surprisingly small and did not match his sexual bravado. Had that been the reason for his rejection? How many long-haired women had he really been with? I asked him why he never made sexual advances before. "I wanted to," he said, "but I didn't want to ruin your life."

He fell asleep. I got up, walked in the dark through the house to the studio, looked at his art, breathing in turpentine, paint, linseed oil, and all the things he'd taught me.

# Blow Up

Arlene called and asked me to go with her to the Red Dog dance club in Scottsdale. She wanted to meet Mr. Clean, the black R&B singer from L.A. who was performing there. We hadn't seen each other since the abortion except for the time a month ago when we played tennis at the abandoned Jokake Inn, where the courts were overgrown with weeds and yellow wildflowers. She apologized, told me she was grateful I'd helped her, and asked if we could be friends again. After hitting a perfect backhand, I said I'd give it a try.

The Red Dog was decorated like an old saloon with sawdust on the floor and western art on the walls. Local and southern California singers like Waylon Jennings played there regularly.

Since I'd known her, Arlene wanted to have sex with a black man. She'd seen a picture of Mr. Clean in the newspaper. His muscle-y body and bald head turned her on.

Mr. Clean wore a billowing white shirt unbuttoned to his navel and tight, striped pants. I wondered if they were stuffed. I'd read Tom Jones padded himself when he performed. Mr. Clean's voice was forceful but lacked the nuance and subtlety of Tom's.

When the band took a break, Arlene went on stage, introduced herself to Mr. Clean, and brought him to our table. He told us his real name was Ollie McClay and he'd played football for the Dallas Cowboys until he injured his back. That's when he started his singing career. He was surprised the audience at the Red Dog was so white.

Arlene positioned her cleavage in his direction. "What, you don't like white girls?"

"Depends on the girl," he said.

Ollie asked me for a date after Arlene went to the bathroom. Why tell her? I'd not seen a body like Ollie's.

"Mind if I touch your arm?"

"Please," he said. His bicep was a smooth rock. My hand slid off his skin. He didn't turn me on, but his body was perfect for learning how to render anatomically correct muscles. I told him I was studying art and asked if he'd pose for me. Ollie agreed. He thought I was coming on to him.

When the band resumed playing, a guy came to the table and asked if he could join me. Older than most of the men in the club, he had red, curly hair and a beard. I could tell he was from out of town. He offered me a cigarette, and I slipped one out of his pack. He popped open his lighter, and I cupped my left hand around his, inhaling deeply as tobacco singed then grew red hot. Arlene and I had practiced cupping each other's hands around a lit match. We thought it gave a sexual signal so we only did it with guys we liked.

Ray was a costume designer from L.A., in town working on the film *Zabriskie Point*. He said he'd been wardrobe shopping at Saks Fifth Avenue that day for Mark Frechette and Daria Halprin, the stars of the movie. I told him my mother worked there in the sportswear department.

"What's her name?"

"Gail."

"She's the one who helped me. She told me about you. She said you're an artist and you might be interested in being an extra in the film. She gave me your number. And here you are. Would you like to dance?"

Ollie was singing the Smokey Robinson song "Tears of a Clown." Ray leaned his body into mine. I put my arm around him. My spine lengthened as I took him in. The collar of his crisp white shirt smelled like limes. His black leather jacket felt like soft wax under my hand. We didn't dance so much as stand in one place swaying. He moved with a laid-back confidence, unlike younger guys who couldn't slow down. Ray's beard soothed my cheek. He whispered in my ear, "Tomorrow, Antonioni's going to blow up a house on Winfield Mountain. Would you like to come?"

"I would," I whispered back.

I told Arlene I was leaving with Ray. "Good for you," she said. "I'm going to stay and have another drink with Ollie."

In the Safari Hotel lobby, on the way to Ray's room, we heard distressed, muffled sounds from behind the front desk. The night clerk was on the floor tied up with duct tape over his mouth. The hotel had been robbed. Ray untied him and called the police. Instead of having sex, we spent the next two hours talking to the cops. I liked Ray more, now that I'd seen the way he rushed to the clerk's aid and talked to him in a soothing voice until help arrived.

\*\*\*

One side of Winfield Mountain was bare with scrubby vegetation close to the ground. Antonioni wanted to film from the other side where desert trees grew. Ray introduced me to Daria whose hair hung to her knees. She wore a beaded belt around her tiny waist. Ray told me her mother was a dancer. He explained that detonating the house was a metaphor for the hippie dream of destroying the establishment.

"Antonioni's been traveling all over the states since *Blow Up*, getting background for this film," said Ray. "He thinks America is a very violent country."

"He's right."

Antonioni pulled up in a Jeep wearing all black with a silver buckled leather belt he probably bought in one of the western shops on Fifth Avenue in Scottsdale. He looked older than I thought he would.

The mocked-up ranch house blew to bits as dynamite exploded in stages. Red, hot fireballs grew tails that flicked and burned through the swimming pool, blasted the kitchen and the outdoor patio to pieces, turning beach towels, furniture, and female mannequins in bikinis with cigarettes glued in their mouths to smoky ash.

I let go of Ray's hand and walked as close to the flames as I could. I imagined a painting, twelve-by-seven feet, of a standing woman encircled by leaping, orange flames and black smoke, untouched by the destruction around her.

\*\*\*

I became Ray's girlfriend and went on location with him and the film crew. We went to Death Valley and from its moon-cratered landscape looked up at stars, pulsing specks of brilliant light. We stayed in cabins a few miles away in the snow-covered town of Lone Pine, named after a lonely pine tree found in a canyon near there. Venison burgers were the favorite dish of the locals.

In Las Vegas, we stayed at the new Circus Circus Hotel and Casino. Ray and I sat at the blackjack table as trapeze artists performed high-flying acts above us. As we played, the memory of Jack gambling away my mother's inheritance surfaced. I told Ray the story and started to shake.

"If I stay here any longer, I'll have a panic attack," I said.

"Let's go." He put his arm around me and led me to the street. We walked to a casino-less restaurant and had dinner.

I liked sleeping with Ray. My skin relaxed, became moist and porous. Maybe it was because he was seventeen years older, but I felt something different when his slightly weathered hands touched me—something besides an urgent insistence for sex. My mind didn't completely trust him, but my body did, and I started to like myself better when I was with him. I didn't know why, but sometimes I'd cry when he left for work.

Antonioni was emotional but quiet, and sometimes mean. One night during a dinner party, a cat climbed his leg and jumped on the table. He threw it across the room when the hostess of the party wasn't looking. He had a thin smile when he was in a good mood and made jokes in Italian.

He exuded the elements in his films, especially *Blow Up*: secretiveness, long silences, trickery, loneliness, blank spaces, and surreal beauty. When I saw *Blow Up*, I knew my purpose was to be a director. Before I started to study painting, seriously, I took hundreds of photographs of odd-angled images, always questioning my vision until I saw the same perspective I had seen in *Blow Up*. Directing would be a natural progression. My mother introduced me to a producer she knew who laughed at me, said there was no such thing as a woman director and there never would be. "The closest you'll ever get is working in a studio as a secretary," he said.

Now, Antonioni was sitting beside me eating Mexican food. I showed him how to stuff tacos with meat, cilantro, lettuce, salsa, and cheese. He watched through smoky-lensed cat-eye glasses, copying me precisely and methodically with his nervous fingers. Later that evening I taught him how to play Gin Rummy. During our game he said, "People talk too much. I don't believe in words."

"I agree," I said. Other than taco and card game instructions, I didn't know what to say to him. *If you want to be a director, you should try to impress him*, I thought. But I hadn't done anything significant to impress him or anyone else.

We traveled to Berkeley so Antonioni could film the student riots. One day he filmed a Black Panther meeting, led by Kathleen Cleaver, in one of the classrooms on campus. Kathleen's husband, Eldridge Cleaver, was one of the founders of the Black Panthers. Antonioni asked me to be in the scene as one of the college students. The meeting was about how they were going to shut down the university. There were guns stacked up on a table, probably props, I thought, but somebody said they were loaded. I sat at a desk in jeans and a turquoise East Indian shirt with tiny mirrors scattered down the front. I crossed my arms over my chest and tried to look as angry as everyone else in the room. I glanced at Ray, who stood beside one of the cameramen. He'd given me some weed beforehand. He said the Black Panthers were militant. No one knew what would happen. They wore black wrap-around shades, black turtlenecks, black leather jackets, African necklaces made of beads the size of knuckles, and black berets cocked on one side of their big Afros. *How many bobby pins did they use?* I thought.

"If there's going to be a revolution, there needs to be a revolutionary party," said Kathleen. At first I thought she was a white woman with an Afro. Her small, heart-shaped face had a sweet look and her teeth were small like a child's. The two front ones crossed and protruded slightly. When she spoke, her striking pale blue eyes darted around the room mischievously. Her light, honey-brown skin glistened under the hot lights. "We no longer accept whitey's values," she said. "We now claim our own heritage." Everyone in the room applauded.

"Right on," they shouted. Had they planned ahead of time to start the revolutionary riot on camera? That seemed like a good idea, but I hoped not. Antonioni didn't give any direction. He let the scene happen.

I didn't want to be part of whitey's system either, but I couldn't be a Black Panther.

Kathleen smoothed her left hand lightly over her Afro. "Our members have no money, no property. Imagination is the most powerful weapon we have."

At midnight, Antonioni ended the scene without incident. The Panthers put the guns in a big wooden crate and carried it away. Ray offered to walk Kathleen to her car. I was surprised she accepted the offer from a white man. One of her tires had been slashed. "This is typical," she said.

Kathleen and I watched Ray change her tire. I'd never met anyone like her: outspoken, courageous, and politically smart. I didn't know what to say. Finally, she said she liked my necklace of three roses carved out of blond pine.

"Ray picked it out for Daria to wear in the Death Valley

scenes," I said. "You know that thing you said about imagination being a weapon? I like that."

"Don't forget it!" she said as she got in her car and drove into the damp night.

The filming of *Zabriskie Point* ended, and I didn't see Antonioni again. If I couldn't be a director, at least I'd gotten closer than working as a secretary in a studio.

***

Ray and I spent Christmas together in Phoenix. I took him to the desert at dawn. When he woke up in the morning, the creases sprouting from around his hazel eyes were more pronounced. As the sun came up, we smoked marijuana, drank coffee, and made love on a flat, gray rock. I liked the weight of his stocky body on mine, and the feeling of his reddish-brown chest and leg hair grazing my skin. I made a collage portrait of him with oil paint, wood, and white silky pampas grass plumes. I gave it to him for Christmas along with a Corn Dancer Kachina doll. A month later, my dog, Boris, and I moved to Nichols Canyon in Hollywood to live with him.

Ray said I could do anything I wanted to make the house my own. I wondered if he'd let me turn the garage into a studio. He'd lived alone for years. The house looked ragged, so I hired a painter to paint inside and out. I showed him how to drag streaks of gray paint along the dark wooden beams in the living room with a sponge so the ceiling would look higher. On the bedroom wall near the sliding glass door, I did a mural of weeping willow trees and Mexican sage. I designed it to look like an extension of the plants, including the marijuana that grew outside on the patio.

I felt confident fixing up the house, but when I met

Ray's friends, I felt out of my element. The first time I met Jim and Shelley, who lived in Laurel Canyon, they were sunbathing nude by the pool, their shiny, wrinkled fifty-year-old bodies gleaming with suntan oil. They wore fat sunglasses and big smiles as they passed me a joint. Hot pink plastic margarita glasses sat on a table wedged between their two lounge chairs. Jim had a little cloth covering his penis. He lifted it for me to see.

"Have to be careful of the sun after sex," he said and laughed. When they asked me to take off my clothes and join them, I said, "Maybe another time." After Ray and I left, I was relieved when he apologized for their weirdness. "But they're in the business."

When Morgana King—the jazz singer whose new album, "I Know How It Feels To Be Lonely," had just come out—came to visit Ray, she wore a hot pink and orange silk caftan that flowed like a flimsy tent over her sizable body. She demanded I make her two pots of Earl Grey tea with lemon and honey. "I have to drink several cups a day to protect my voice," she said.

I liked Barb, the former wife of the saxophone player, Gerry Mulligan. She was a small, wiry woman who threw parties with jazz musicians I'd never heard of. She made a point of introducing me. She chain-smoked and flitted around the room, making sure everyone was comfortable. Ray told everyone I was an artist. Unsure how people would react to my work, I didn't hang anything on the walls at the house until Barb came over one day and raved about the mural in the bedroom.

I pretended I was used to sunbathing nude with strangers, serving tea to divas, and hanging out with famous musicians. Most of the time I felt like a hick from Arizona, but I'd had lots of practice reading people and adjusting to new situations. In this case, I did my best to act sophisticated and like I knew something about the movie business. I imitated what I saw as Hollywood gestures; I smoked dramatically—I'd always known how to do that; I rolled my eyes and nodded my head and said things like "Honestly!" or "Can you believe it!" when someone made a derogatory comment about someone, having assessed that these were key phrases. It didn't matter if I didn't know whom they were talking about or that I sounded like my mother. Fake it until you make it was my mantra.

When I got up my nerve, I'd express a mild opinion about something and see how it went over. I didn't want to embarrass Ray. I drank Scotch, margaritas, or wine, and I dressed like a movie version of a hippie or an artist in expensive copies of shirts from India, hippie beads, and bellbottoms. Ray brought home clothes and jewelry from his movies. Eventually, I hoped to feel accepted.

\*\*\*

On our vacation to Puerto Vallarta, we stayed at the Oceano Hotel, famous for its bar, where Elizabeth Taylor and Richard Burton drank when they were in town. We went to Yalapa in a rickety boat and ate turtle meat at an open-air stand. We saw the island of Mismaloya where *Night of the Iguana* was shot. Ray said he wished he'd done the costumes for that film. I'd watched him prepare for a job. He'd devour art books and photographs, memorize the script, read it aloud to me.

"Costumes paint a character's portrait, show their status, occupation, and attitude," he said. One Sunday at Warner Bros. studio, I watched him age several pairs of jeans for a Western with a gray-colored stone and some kind of liquid solution that smelled like eggs. The process reminded me of removing unwanted layers on a canvas by scraping into wet oil paint. Ray used color, line, and texture like I did. Despite the difference in our ages, we had a similar sensibility.

After a few days in Mexico, I got diarrhea from drinking the water and eating speared fish sold by children on the beach. I tried medicines from the pharmacy but nothing worked.

"I'll go score some weed," said Ray. "Sometimes it's the only thing that helps." He came back to the hotel an hour later. He propped pillows behind my head and sat on the bed rubbing my shoulder while I smoked a joint. Ray was right. The diarrhea stopped.

"There you go, baby," he said. "See how well I take care of you?"

A place in me stiffened. I felt myself falling into a wide net of protection. I wanted to rest there, but no matter how slack the webbing, it was still a net and I knew how the spaces could shrink.

"It's not like I need that much," I said. A salt-air breeze came through the window. I closed my eyes. The mariachi band downstairs in the bar began to sing "El Reloj." I dreamed I was lying alone on a beach in Havana surrounded by saxophones, horns, a bass guitar, and drums, arranged in the sand like the structures at Stonehenge. The instruments began to play, gleaming and sparkling in the sun. The figure of a man stood in the distance as I moved to the music like a wet hunk of seaweed undulating in the sand.

\*\*\*

Back in L.A., Ray became enamored with the song "The Folks Who Live on the Hill." He played the record constantly, singing along with Patti Page.

"That's us, honey," he'd say. "Maybe someday there'll be three of us on the hill."

"You're kidding."

"You don't want kids?" Ray sat next to me on the couch, lit a joint, and passed it to me.

"Do you?" This could ruin everything. I inhaled the smoke deep into my lungs. I couldn't imagine someone invading my body, sucking, needy, dependent on me for survival.

"Not for sure," Ray said. He looked into my eyes, then turned and stared out the sliding glass door to the patio.

"I'm not ready for that," I said.

Ray took my hand and squeezed it. He smiled. "You don't have to be."

After that, he surprised me with gifts: paintbrushes, expensive linen canvases, embroidered Mexican blouses, and shiny beaded earrings. He told me he loved me with or without kids. I began to feel a creeping sense of unnamable dread. I wanted to stay with Ray, so I pretended it wasn't there. My mistrust of men had been finely honed in childhood. I'd loved them, and they'd all left. Could I break my habit of distance and allow Ray to take care of me? Maybe. But I could never do the kid thing.

\*\*\*

Ray left town to work on a film in Europe, and I stayed in the house alone. I rummaged through everything like a detective, hoping to find a sign that would tell me whether or not I should stay with him. I didn't find any secrets except for a stack of soft-porn magazines in the garage, which wasn't a sign to leave.

It was the summer of the first moon landing. I took pictures of the TV screen as Apollo 11 landed and Neil Armstrong stepped onto the moon. It didn't seem real.

A month later, Sharon Tate and her unborn baby were murdered at her house on Cielo Drive in Benedict Canyon, minutes away from Ray's house. After Charles Manson's followers killed her, they wrote PIG in her blood on the front door. The next night, they went to the La Biancos' house and murdered them. Over the course of two days, they killed four others.

Many celebrities left town. There were rumors that other members of the Manson family were combing the hills, hiding out, waiting for orders to strike again. Barb learned that Manson and his followers liked to break into people's houses and re-arrange the furniture to mess with their minds.

The morning after the murders, I saw a construction worker shoveling dirt on the lot above the house with his fly open and his penis swinging with the movement of his shovel. Was he a cult member? I kept my eye on him from the bedroom window. He seemed to know when I was watching. He'd stop shoveling and look in my direction.

That afternoon he came down the hill with his penis hanging out. He knocked on the bedroom door and asked for a glass of water. Boris growled in low undertones, ready to attack. His back hair spiked straight up. I told the guy he could drink water from the hose. I ran to the living room and locked the sliding glass doors. Boris stood with his nose to the glass, barking so hard his legs moved him backwards across the wood floor. I hid in the kitchen. The marijuana was growing thick and high on the patio so I couldn't call the cops. After drinking for a long while and peering into the house, he dropped the hose, left the water running, went back up the hill, and disappeared. I didn't see him again, but for days afterwards I was sure I heard the sound of a spade hitting dry rocky ground.

Ray called from Italy.

"Are you all right?"

"I'm fine, but I was thinking I should get a gun. Do you have one?"

"Of course not."

"I've been around guns, you know."

"I want you to get out of there." His voice crackled. "Those Manson people could be nearby."

"I'm starting a new painting class." I took the phone with me to the patio door and locked it.

"Please leave the house."

"I can hardly hear you."

"Go see your family in Phoenix until I come back," he yelled.

"I don't want to miss the class, and besides I have Boris." I didn't tell him about the man.

"That dog can't protect you. I love you."

I twisted the phone cord around my wrist. Sometimes Ray acted like I imagined a father would, although I had no clue what a father-daughter relationship was like.

"Can you hear me? When I get back there's something important I want to ask you. Will you call me every day and let me know you're okay?"

"All right," I shouted before we were disconnected.

I knew Ray wanted to propose. That night, I awoke to whispering noises coming from the patio. Boris growled. I stayed in bed and it stopped a few minutes later, but I didn't sleep all night. Boris lay beside me with his head resting on my chest.

# The Three Times I Saw My Father

For my high school graduation, my father, who left when I was three and Kimberly was one, sent me a wrist corsage, a chunk of white flowers I didn't recognize surrounding one red rose. It came in a frosty box, tied with a pink ribbon, and the message on the card read, *Congratulations. Love, Bud.* I wondered how he knew I was graduating and how he'd found me living at my grandmother's house in Phoenix. She and my mother hated him, and, as far as I knew, hadn't spoken to him since my parents' divorce. Growing up, my mother told me he would have made a lousy father so it was a good thing he wasn't around.

"He sees women as either virgins or whores," she'd said, "and he only married me because I wouldn't sleep with him." I guess he liked the whores better. He had an affair with a nightclub singer named Phyllis, and when my mother found out, she divorced him. My grandmother called him a bum and told me he'd never paid a dime in child support.

I didn't remember a thing about him. Then, after fifteen years, there he was in a flower box, provoking me to unpack an abandonment I'd kept hidden deep in a crevice of my gut like a stone sitting by a river.

I wanted to send the flowers back. But there was no return address, and I had no idea where he lived. My grandmother put the unopened box in the refrigerator in case I wanted to open it later. She didn't like anything to go to waste. When the petals turned brown, I threw the corsage in the trash.

The longing for my father began at age twenty and became chronic three months before I turned twenty-one. About to cross over into adulthood, I was trying to decide if I should stay with Ray, my first serious relationship. We'd been living together for a year. He was, however, seventeen years older than I was, and I feared I'd chosen a father figure.

I knew self-assured women whose fathers had been in their lives at every step. Would my life have been different, better or worse, if my father had been there for me? By the time I was twelve, I'd had two step-fathers, even taken their last names at my mother's insistence. They only stayed for the duration of the marriages, two and three years. At this point, my father couldn't help me with life decisions, but like an adopted person, I felt drawn to, seduced by, biology.

While Ray was in Europe, I called my mother to ask if she had my father's address.

"I can't imagine why in God's name you'd want to contact him," she said, "but I have his sister Marge's address in Chicago. I suppose you could write to her."

Marge wrote back right away, told me to write my father a letter, that I should send it to her and she'd make sure he got it.

I sat at the glass dining room table, looking out through an overcast sky at the spotted hills. Some were green with ice plants, others patched with brown from last summer's fire. Mourning doves cooed on the back deck. I smoked cigarettes as I thought of what to say. I took deep drags and began to write fast and hard with a squeaky felt tip pen. My hand jerked across the page.

*Dear Bud,*

*I'm writing because I'd like to see you. I don't know if you're interested in seeing me, since you've never made the effort. Haven't you been curious about your own daughters? Maybe you're scared, but I would like to have some sense of who you are. All I know is what Mother has told me over the years. I gave my phone number to Marge.*

*Your daughter,*
*Linda*

I lit another cigarette and threw the match into the ashtray. For a second the flame caught on an accordion muffin paper left over from what I'd eaten earlier. I addressed the letter and pulled on a pair of jeans. I drove to the post office, down the hill, still in the T-shirt I'd slept in, hair uncombed, face unwashed. On the way back to the house, I bought an early birthday cake with yellow flowers. I ate slice after slice with chocolate ice cream.

\*\*\*

Two weeks later my father called. He talked as if he wasn't familiar with the telephone, with no extra words or conversation. His voice receded back into the phone and further back into his throat. He said he lived near L.A. and suggested we meet on Saturday at noon at the Radar Room on Santa Monica Boulevard. I'd driven past the non-descript dive of a tavern that opened at six in the morning, a little neon Budweiser logo flashed off and on in the blackened window. I thought my father would invite me out to lunch or at least to a nice bar.

I arrived first. The place was dark and empty, except for the bartender and an older man and woman sitting at the end of the bar in matching plaid shirts. I sat on a stool facing the red Naugahyde door. Gold buttons punched every few inches into its skin.

After a few minutes, the door swung open. He stood in a cloud of glaring light. I made an awning with my hand above my eyebrows and squinted to refocus. He had a gangly look. I'd known all my life he was exactly six-foot-four.

I remembered a photograph of him taken when he was twenty-two. The picture shows his face in sunlight, his eyes half-closed, his blond hair slicked back, holding me away from his body. He appears to be either presenting me to the camera as a gift, or desperate for someone to take me from him. I could never tell which.

I stood up, and he came toward me.

"Linda?" he said, extending his hand.

I was afraid he might hug me or try to kiss me and maybe cry. It was a good thing he didn't do any of those things. I might have had feelings I couldn't control, and he hadn't earned the right to see any of that.

He wore loose black pants and a white T-shirt. I'd seen the same outfit in an old golf picture my mother showed me once. He held his neck and head to the right. He must have had the same slight scoliosis in his back that I had. I smelled liquor on his breath.

We sat at the bar. He ordered a beer and lit a cigarette with his big Zippo lighter. His hands shook, and he had broken capillaries on his cheeks. I was glad I didn't look like him in the face with his thin jaw and tight little ears too close to his head. We had the same shade of blond hair.

When I pulled out a cigarette, he clicked open the Zippo. He held it out to me with his long fingers. A wiggly bluish flame popped up.

"So, you smoke? Does your mother allow you to smoke and live with a man?"

"What gave you the idea I live with a man?"

"How else could a girl your age be living in the Hollywood Hills? You're not even twenty-one," he said.

"That's what you have to say after all these years?"

"No." He brushed ashes from his black pants, making whitish streaks down his legs.

"Well, you're wrong," I lied. "And as far as smoking goes, it's a little late for you to have an opinion." I took a dramatic drag on my cigarette and let the smoke escape slowly from my mouth. I drummed my nails on the black fake leather roll wrapped around the edge of the bar top.

"What about college?"

"I'm planning to go to art school." I thought he might be impressed.

He looked down and shook his head. "Better find yourself a good husband."

"You're kidding, right?"

"It's hard to make it in the arts. That's all I'm saying."

"How would you know?"

"Never mind. I'm sorry. Forget I said anything."

"Believe me, I will." I blew smoke in his direction.

"I'd like to invite you to my house this afternoon." He clasped his hand over his lighter and looked straight ahead. "How are your mother and Kimberly?"

"Fine, I guess."

"Will you come?"

I took a deep breath. "Where do you live?"

"In Reseda." He put his cigarette in the ashtray and rubbed his forehead. "Come and meet Phyllis."

I had to see the "floozy," as my mother called her. "All right. I'll follow you."

\*\*\*

His apartment building was near a park with well-groomed grass, flowers, Eucalyptus trees, and picnic tables. He lived in a stucco building. The small pool wasn't very clean and there were faint rust stains on the front of his unit.

One wall of his living room was covered in mirror squares, streaked with a wavy pattern of gold lines. A pale blue sofa, worn in the middle. A dusty white baby grand piano looked out of place in the corner.

Holding two bottles of beer, the floozy stood in the doorway that separated the kitchen from the living room. My father took one of the beers. Her hand trembled as she offered me the other.

"You're so tall," she said.

She was a younger, shorter version of my mother with more make-up. We sat down on the sofa and drank our beers. Phyllis told me she worked as a nurse. She fell in love with my father one night in a bar in Calumet City when she heard him play "After You're Gone."

"Your father plays terrific piano. Play something for her, Bud."

"She doesn't want that, Phil. She's angry. She thinks it's all my fault. Show her the letters."

Phyllis went to the hall closet. When she opened it, little sweaters, booties, and rattles floated out and tumbled to her feet. She explained that these were things left over from the three times she'd miscarried. "I've never been able to throw them away."

I looked at my father. Above his head I saw myself and Phyllis reflected back in mirrored pieces, slashed with gold.

"Here they are." She handed me a box.

"I don't want it. Really I don't."

"You didn't want me," said my father. "The proof is in those letters from you and Kimberly. You wanted that third husband of your mother's to legally adopt you."

"A woman from the court told us we had to write them. I was only ten. I didn't know who the hell you were. I still don't. Whose fault is that? And it never happened. They divorced before the adoption was final, which you would have known if you'd bothered to stay in touch and done something all these years besides send me a stupid wrist corsage."

I took the dusty Capezio shoebox from Phyllis and threw it across the room. My mother's lemon-colored envelopes scattered through the air as I left Phyllis standing at the hall closet up to her ankles in dead baby clothes and my father on the sofa mumbling, "Just like her mother."

Soon after, I decided Ray was too set in his ways and I left him.

\*\*\*

Twelve years later, when Ben asked me to marry him, I again felt pulled to see my father. I hadn't wanted him to meet any of the other men I'd been with—the Mexican opera singer who I found out had read my mail and spied on me, the sixty-year-old Brazilian flamenco guitar player, the married president of an art school, the Texas oilman with a drug problem, the Vanderbilt heir who wore a bad toupee and started drinking at ten in the morning, the seventy-year-old movie director, or the gay dancer I fell in love with who I thought might turn for me.

Ben was neither wealthy nor interested in the arts, but a calm, grounded body worker, a Rolfer, who used his hands to align people's bodies. I felt safe with him, and he was my age.

I'd squelched all fantasies of a wedding, a walk down the aisle with a dad. But my biology believed that seeing my father again and introducing him to Ben would help me make the right decision. My mind said, *Forget it. This is crazy. He's a pathetic drunk.*

My mother told me she'd heard that Phyllis had divorced him. He'd moved to Rancho Mirage and was working as a tax accountant. "You know, in college he was considered a genius at math."

I'd never heard that before. I'd always had trouble with math.

"I hope to God you get this out of your system," she said.

"I hope so too, Mother."

I decided to make the trip alone, check out my father's condition before I brought Ben to meet him.

His stone house on Terrace Road was the only one in the neighborhood that hadn't been remodeled. Dusty rose paint had peeled and hung in strips on the front of the house. In the yard, a chewed-up cactus garden of barrel and saguaro was trying to stay alive. A mailman's Jeep was parked in the driveway.

As I got out of the car, the early afternoon sun poured over me. I walked to the door and heard piano music. I stood there and listened. It sounded like a recording, and then I realized it must be my father playing a jazz version of "Ebb Tide." I'd never heard anything like it. My scalp began to perspire. A small rusty wind-bell hung over my head. I took a deep breath, found the round brass buzzer, and pushed.

The music stopped, and I heard him cough. He opened the door. He was heavier since I'd seen him last, and his face was scarlet. He shook my hand and started to cry. I didn't know what to do. He wiped his bloodshot eyes with the bottom of his T-shirt, exposing his puffed-out, white belly.

He guided me to the kitchen.

The floor was dark green, sticky linoleum. I stood behind him while he opened the refrigerator. I saw a pint of milk, a case of beer, and a package of yellow cheese. He handed me a can of beer, and I followed him to the living room. Little bits of foam from the couch cushion poked out as I sat down. He sat at an upright piano that was shoved against a wall in a little alcove off the kitchen. He put the beer on the piano bench between his legs.

"How was the drive?" he asked.

"The freeway was wide open."

My father wiped his eyes again.

Were his tears for me?

"How's the art career?"

"Great. My work hangs in a few galleries now." It was only one but I wouldn't tell him that. I wondered if he'd ever tried to make a living as a musician. I lit a cigarette.

"Still smoking?" he asked.

I wanted to scream. I tried to calm myself by looking away, but all I saw out the back window was a swimming pool, half-full of brown water, covered with dead palm fronds from the shriveled date trees.

"I have to use the bathroom," I said.

As I walked down the hallway, I spotted an old man in a mailman's uniform in one of the bedrooms. He sat on the bed looking down at several pieces of mail stacked in the middle of the floor. He lifted his hand in a wave.

The bathroom hadn't been cleaned in a long time. The light didn't come on when I flipped the switch. I held myself up with one hand on the back of the toilet where an assortment of dirty seashells had been arranged on a piece of coral shag carpeting, no doubt by some girlfriend who'd had domestic ideas. Returning to the living room, I noticed the mailman was gone, the mail still on the floor.

"Who's that guy down the hall?" I asked.

"My roommate. We were in the war together." He turned toward the keyboard. "You know, I used to play an awful lot of boogie."

The sun peeked over the backside of the house, and a small square of light hit his anklebone.

"Most songs I learned off of records. This one is my own. Never picked it up from anyone."

*Had he ever written music for me?*

His hands came down hard, and his fingers began to slide over the keys, his arms gliding, wrists loose, hands flying through the air, fingers flopping down, hitting the right keys with each stroke, his feet bouncing under the piano hitting the pedals, wild, like Jerry Lee Lewis. When he was younger, he must have brought the house down.

He finished playing, and I didn't know what to do but clap.

"My hands and arms aren't what they used to be. I can't play those basses anymore. Those are complicated. But I tried. I used to play all kinds of songs, 'Walking Bass Man Boogie,' 'Sleepy Time Down South,' 'Mood Indigo,' lots of things."

"Did you play when I was little?" I asked.

"I've always played. In high school, my friends used to take me down to the beer parlor. I won't tell you how old I was. I was much too young to be drinking. This one's called 'After You're Gone.'"

As he started to play, I walked over to the piano and watched. I stood as close as I could without touching him. I wanted to take in his breath. As he played harder, I felt a drop of his sweat spray onto my skin. I had a crazy thought. What if I licked my arm, tasted him? I'd seen Muhammad Ali's trainer do that once. Someone told me that by tasting Ali's sweat, the trainer could tell what vitamins and minerals his body was lacking. Maybe if I tasted my father's sweat, I would know him.

When he finished playing, he turned to me. "Well, that was probably worth one beer anyway."

I asked him what he played when he and my mother were together.

"Lots of things." And then as if I weren't there, he gazed out the window with wet cheeks and reminisced about the times he spent in New York City, in Greenwich Village and on 52nd Street. He said he used to go there on weekends, and it was quite an experience. As he was talking, he wiped the sweat off his beer can and then rubbed his calf. "Billie Holiday sang there. Art Tatum played the piano. Albert Johnson. All the great ones."

My mother had told me she thought she'd be happy married to my father. On their honeymoon, they stopped in Greenwich Village. Both of them wanted to stay there and be artists: she an actress and he a jazz pianist. Instead, they went back to live in Chicago, and he ended up working for her father.

"In one of those clubs, I got to know these two colored guys. I used to sit in with them once in a while," Bud said. He went to the kitchen to get another beer before coming back to the piano to play again.

As he became lost in the music once again, I realized the impossibility of bonding with him. My father's life of sadness, failure, and regret permeated my body. I hoped this wasn't genetic. I had to get away from him. He would never meet Ben. I walked to the couch and picked up my purse. I looked inside for a tissue. "It's late," I said. "I should go."

"So soon? Well, before you do ..." He got up and handed me a stack of small papers from the top of the piano. "A few gas receipts, Union 76. In case you need more car expense deductions. If you ever have any tax questions, give me a call."

"Thanks," I said. I could hardly move. My blood felt thick, like quicksand. I held onto the doorframe to steady myself as my father grasped my other hand with both of his.

Tears pooled in his blue eyes. "Well, Linda ... have a good one."

"Well, bye," I said, letting go of his hands. I stepped outside, squinting into the glare of the late afternoon sun.

\*\*\*

Ten years later, the stability and safety I'd felt with Ben had gradually become a prison of control. Soon after my divorce, I moved into an apartment in Los Feliz. I paid the first and last month's rent with money I'd made selling my artwork. If I was careful, I had enough to last for the next few months.

One day, Mr. Haas, the social worker at the Soldiers and Sailors Veterans home in Quincy, Illinois, called to tell me my father was dying of bone cancer. "We've been having some talks," he said. "Your father realizes he made some bad choices. He's on morphine and pretty much incoherent, but he wants to see you. I called your mother and sister. They don't want anything to do with him."

I crossed my legs tight. My right foot started to shake. I couldn't deal with any more grief. I'd unpacked that abandonment stone from my stomach again and again with no resolution.

"I'll have to think about it," I said.

"He only has a few days."

He didn't deserve my being there. I couldn't afford a plane ticket, but I didn't want to regret not going. A crooked branch from the Indigo bush outside the picture window in the dining room scratched back and forth on the glass. My new cat, Camilla, who'd found her way into the apartment through an cracked-open window, jumped in my lap.

"All right, I'll be there," I said.

I hung up the phone and paced the shiny blond wood floor, holding Camilla like a baby.

\*\*\*

Mr. Haas, whose first name was Bob, picked me up at the Quincy Regional Airport the next day. He wore large-lens, black-framed glasses, earmuffs, and a down jacket with some stains on the front, probably from food he'd eaten in his car. He said the town was named for John Quincy Adams. I told him my mother had gone to school nearby at Lindenwood College for Women. I hadn't bothered to tell her about the trip.

Bob drove on a slick highway surrounded on either side by bluish-white ground, hard from layers of snow and ice that had frozen into each other. Midwestern trees that I would never see green and flowering stood in the earth like oddly shaped stick statues, roots below ice, below freezing.

"If the nurses seem unfriendly, it's because they have a hard time when relatives don't come until someone is ready to die."

"He's never been part of my life," I said.

"I told them it goes both ways."

*I've come for myself*, I thought. *To finally end the longing.*

We drove through the gray brick-columned entrance under the *Soldiers and Sailors Home* sign that curved in an arc above us. An uneven wrought-iron fence enclosed the grounds, sloping with the lay of the land. The place was its own town. We passed buildings that looked like barracks scattered around 200 acres of snow and ice-packed land. Bob pointed out the pharmacy, mess hall, bank, and museum.

"There's the lake," he said pointing one leather-gloved finger to the left. "It's in the shape of Illinois. It's frozen over now. We have beautiful swans in the summertime." He pulled into the parking lot of Fletcher Hall Infirmary, where my father lived. "Be careful walking. It's slick."

We went through the smoking area where a group of about thirty vets sat in wheelchairs, some with missing legs, whispering to each other through stagnant yellowish air.

"That's Bud's daughter."

"Hey, good-looking."

A few of them wolf whistled.

The smoke stung my eyes. Inside the building smelled rancid, full of the kind of sickness and death I'd never seen. I walked fast, looked straight ahead over the heads of the wounded men.

On the way to my father's room, I thought of telling him that I'd stopped smoking. But now he probably wouldn't understand anything I said.

A woman with outstretched arms rushed toward me in the hallway. "I'm your Aunt Marge," she said. She introduced me to her husband, Ed. He shook my hand. She squeezed me hard. I kept my body stiff as she patted her right hand up and down on my back. "You're as tall as I am." She acted like she knew me. She seemed genuinely kind. I wanted to feel some immediate kinship, but I didn't.

We all went to my father's room. He was squirming around in a twin bed that was too short for his six-foot-four body.

He sat up and said, "My Linda."

I felt my heart pound through my veins. I sucked my chest in as far as I could, pushing down forty-two years of yearning that now wanted to come pouring out. I could barely breathe.

Marge, Ed, Bob, and Sandi, my father's nurse, all gasped. They couldn't believe he recognized me. Then he started to squirm and moan again. He was naked. A small sheet covered his torso and thighs. A stuffed lion with a red bow around its neck sat next to his pillow, a gift from Sandi.

She told me how much everyone loved my father, how when he played the piano it seemed to have a healing effect on the men.

"They'd all sing. And your dad was funny," she said in her southern accent. "He made everyone laugh. We think the world of him. It must be driving him crazy to be confined to a bed. He was always so restless, up and down during the night, outside smoking."

They left me alone with him. I sat by the side of his too-short deathbed and held his hand for the first time. His fingers were shaped like mine—long, with smooth knuckles. He had no gray hair. His shiny eyes rolled as his head jerked back and forth on the pillow.

"I wish you'd been around," I whispered to him.

"Buddy is dying," he said. "You're beautiful. Who are you?"

I looked around his doorless cubicle that contained a tiny sink, a closet about two feet wide, the bed, a metal chair, and a night table that held a radio and some pill bottles. There were no photographs. He shared a large room with three other men, each with their own separate living cube. There must have been a community bathroom, but I didn't know where it was.

I tuned the radio to a jazz station, thinking my father would like to hear the music he loved. I recognized the Bill Evans Trio from the sixties. Dexter Gordon was on the saxophone. I wondered if my father knew about these musicians. Maybe they were after his time.

He thrashed around, jerking his body from one side of the bed to the other.

"I've got to get to know those girls," he said.

Hungry for any fragment of recognition that I could construe as love, I pulled his words into my body.

He kicked the sheet to the floor.

I saw his penis laying slack against his leg. It was pink, purple at the tip. I stared at it until a nurse I hadn't seen before came in and covered him up. She glared at me and then, with a shotglass in her hand, poured two ounces of bourbon into a paper cup. "The doctor prescribed it for him," she said. "Because of his alcoholism." She lifted the cup to his chapped lips. He sucked it in through a straw. He closed his eyes. For a few minutes he was quiet. The nurse left the room. I laid my hand softly on his chest until I heard Aunt Marge's voice in the hallway. She came in the room with Dr. Beckton. Decisions had to be made about whether my father should be moved to the hospital. Did I want to authorize giving him more morphine?

"Marge should decide," I said.

"You're the next of kin, his daughter. It's up to you," said Dr. Beckton.

My father tried to say something, but we couldn't understand.

"Give him more morphine," I said. "And a bigger bed."

\*\*\*

Marge and Ed took me to dinner that night to the local fish restaurant. The specialty was fried catfish. The dark wood-paneled walls were draped with fish nets. We ordered our dinners from a waitress in a long, blue, fish-print dress.

Marge removed the lemon from her iced tea and took a long gulp. Ed began eating his appetizer, a bowl of catfish soup.

"I know it means a lot to your father that you came," Marge said.

"To us, too," said Ed. "It's too bad Kimberly couldn't come. Did you know you're related to John Smith who came over on the Mayflower?"

"And William Henry Harrison, the ninth president," said Marge. She told me I had another aunt, Edrey, who used to work for Jonas Salk. She was living in Washington with her husband and two children. "What kinds of things do you want to know, honey?"

"What about my father?"

"He was captain of his high school basketball team, voted best athlete at Ellington Field in Texas where he was stationed for a while during the war. Every sport he tried, he was good at."

*Me too,* I thought. I'd been good at ballet, horseback riding, and tennis; Kimberly had been good at modern dance.

Aunt Marge smiled and looked into my eyes. "One day your grandfather, Milton, took him to Beverly Country Club to play golf. Your father had never played before but he was good at it right away. Your mother thought people were impressed with him because he was Milton's son-in-law. Well, your father was great in his own right. He was a wonderful musician. He played by ear."

"I've heard him. I played piano and classical guitar when I was younger."

Our catfish dinners came to the table, served with canned peas, marinated tomatoes, and pale, runny cole-slaw.

"And then, of course, that husband of your mother's adopted you and your sister," said Marge.

"No he didn't. I told Bud."

"Oh. We thought he did. Poor Buddy. He didn't know what to do about that. He consulted a counselor at a church, and she told him not to fight it."

As if he would have. I gazed down and scraped the fried and breaded skin off my fish. Without its coating, the catfish tasted like the scavenger it was.

Suddenly, I saw my father as a blond, skinny boy, the

baby of the family, an ineffectual, excuse-ridden alcoholic, defended and doted on by his big sister. *Poor little Buddy.*

Marge said there were problems in the marriage from the beginning. My grandfather gave my father an accounting job at the trucking company he owned but wouldn't give him a full salary. He put most of my father's earnings into a trust fund for me. For Christmas one year, he gave my father a tie and my mother a new car with her name engraved on the driver's side door.

I pushed my plate away and asked the waitress for a hot toddy.

"And after your dad was charged with manslaughter," Marge said, "he tried so hard to stop drinking. He felt terrible. You were just a baby."

"What? Mother never told me that."

"She was in the car too. They'd both had too much to drink. Your dad swerved off the road and hit a man walking down the side of the highway."

"Did he go to jail?"

"No, thank God. Jail would have killed him. Your grandfather took care of it somehow, and the charge was dismissed. Soon after it happened, we went to a Christmas party at your mom and dad's house. Bud wasn't drinking. He'd started going to A.A. meetings. Your mother kept going up to him, putting a drink under his nose, and laughing. I thought to myself, how can this marriage last?"

"Who was the man?" I asked.

"Oh, we never knew," said Ed.

I looked down at the pieces of ugly fish on my plate and wondered what the man's name had been. Who had he left behind? My father had been twenty-three. He must have thought of it and drank over it every day.

With their heads down, Marge and Ed ate cheesecake

for dessert. I ordered another drink.

***

Outside, as the blue-black night air began to freeze, we drove back to my hotel, passing what looked like a Tiki lounge called the Firehouse Bar, across the street from the side entrance of the veterans home. Marge said my father walked there every day to drink, even the day after his hip surgery. She sent the bartender money each month to water down his drinks.

The next morning I sat in the lobby near the nurse's station waiting for the Sunday service to begin. I asked Aunt Marge what religion she and my father grew up with.

"Christian Science. Your grandfather Royal Senior cured himself of a heart attack sitting in a chair reading Mary Baker Eddy's *Science and Health*."

"I wish I'd known him."

Reverend McCoy arrived, took off his pork-pie hat, and walked over to me. "God is very pleased with you, Linda." During the service he asked everyone to pray for Bud and his family.

Afterward, I went to see my father while Marge and Ed talked to the nurses. They'd given him more morphine.

He turned toward me. His eyes were closed. "Buddy is dead. It's scary."

"It is scary." I kissed him on the cheek.

"It's too late," he said.

"For what?" I waited for another fragment about me.

"To get a few drinks," he said.

My head began to ache. I felt dizzy. I went to the nurse's station and asked Sandi if there was a room somewhere in the building where I could rest. She took me upstairs to a small conference room. On the walls were photographs of vets in uniforms with medals on their chests, standing or kneeling in front of camouflage tanks and helicopters. Miniature cannons on small carriages, their barrels facing outward, were arranged in a perfect circle on the conference table. I moved the chairs back and made a space in the middle of the floor. I locked the door. I put five layers of tissue on the stained carpet for my head, then lay down and sobbed until some of the clutching in my chest subsided.

When I came back to the room, Marge was there. I told her I'd like to have something of my father's. She looked in his closet. There was nothing but a pair of pants, a navy-blue striped shirt, and a pair of bedroom slippers. She took the Timex watch off his wrist and handed it to me. I put it on. The leather watchband smelled like smoke.

She invited me to the mess hall for lunch—grilled cheese sandwiches, and chocolate milkshakes. "We can listen to the jukebox." I told her I wanted to take a walk. She patted my arm and handed me her sheepskin-lined gloves. I walked on snowplowed roads under ice-encrusted tree branches to the Firehouse Bar. It was a wooden building that looked like an island shack with a totem pole in front and Tiki masks on the door. I guessed it was designed to bring back memories for the World War II vets, like my father, who'd spent time in the South Pacific.

I'd planned to go into the Firehouse Bar, sit where my father sat, talk to the bartender, drink whatever the watered-down drink was. But now I thought I'd done enough. I sat on the Tiki god bench by the entrance, flanked by gas-flamed torches, breathing in my father's losses and my own, each one visible for a moment as I exhaled in the cold air.

The temperature dropped, and I walked back to the veterans home. Marge gave me a check for $638, which covered my plane fare. "It was all that was left in your father's bank account. I know he'd want you to have it," she said.

The next morning, Ed drove me to the airport.

My father died that afternoon while I was flying back to Los Angeles. Marge had his body shipped to Mount Greenwood Cemetery, outside of Chicago. He was buried next to his cousin Buzz, who'd been killed in the war.

\*\*\*

I started taking hour-long walks through my new neighborhood, looking at the art deco houses up and down Los Feliz Boulevard, timing myself by my father's watch. After a few weeks the smoke smell disappeared, but even with a new battery, the Timex had stopped working.

# Pink Flamingos

I visited Arlene at the three-bedroom ranch house that she and her boyfriend, Frenchy, had bought on Osborn Road near the old Holiday Inn in Scottsdale. Sitting on a black barstool at the kitchen counter, I looked through the Venetian blinds at the front yard while Arlene, wearing a reddish-brown Afro wig, made margaritas in a blender. Water from the sprinklers made half-circle arcs over the yard, which was bare and smelled of manure. Arlene said Frenchy had just put in the grass.

"I heard you were in town," she'd said on the phone. "Please come over. I want you to see my baby boy. I've missed you."

The last time I saw Arlene, she'd quit her go-go dancing job at the Tradewinds Bar after she met Harry, her seventy-five-year-old, not-so-rich sugar daddy who lived in a double-wide trailer near Tempe. She visited him two or three times a week, kissed his unshaven face, and stuck her tongue in his mouth while warding off further advances. He gave her anywhere between twenty and fifty dollars per visit. She'd bribe me with pot and Benzedrine to go with her as a sexual shield. Harry offered to give me money, too, if we'd have a threesome. I laughed, and he didn't bring it up again.

"Dealing with Harry is easier than warding off the men at the Tradewinds," she said. "A girl has to survive."

I hoped Frenchy could support her and the baby.

"Where is he?" I asked.

"In the bedroom. We can see him later. I need a break. We named him Oliver, Ollie for short," she said.

"Wasn't that the name of the singer at the Red Dog, the club where we used to dance? The guy you had a crush on? I remember doing a painting of him."

"Yeah."

"Are you nursing him?"

"No way."

"I've never seen it done before. I was hoping I could watch," I said.

"Well, it hurt like hell; and I got an infection."

Arlene turned the margarita glasses upside down in a dish of salt, then poured the frothy liquid from the blender. Holding it by its stem, she handed me a glass. I took a sip. Salt and cactus juice burned my throat. I stared at the diamond ring on her finger.

"Cubic Zirconium," she said. "I bought it for myself. No one knows we're not really married. You're the only one I would tell." Arlene sat down on the bar stool next to me and lit a cigarette. She smoked it out of the side of her mouth. "I was looking for a good time. I dug shocking people. You should have seen the looks we got."

"I'll bet. I've never even seen a white woman with a black man in this town."

"I liked making them uncomfortable, but now with Ollie, it's a different story. People come up and call me a nigger lover right to my face. Frenchy's sister, Leona, accused me of getting pregnant on purpose so I could have a brother for myself. So I hit her. I never expected to have a baby with Frenchy, but I couldn't go through another border-town abortion."

*Yeah, neither could I*, I thought.

Arlene sucked smoke deep into her body. Her skin was lined like leather from too much sun. In high school we were always perfectly tanned. During our sunbathing sessions, our bodies shining with baby oil, we held the backs of our hands toward the sun to make sure they matched the rest of us.

"Anyway, Leona hit me back and we got into it. Frenchy's two aunts had to break us up. All those women are on welfare. Well, I won. Leona's nose bled, and I ripped her blouse. She didn't know who she was messing with." Arlene poured herself another margarita. "She thought I was some wimpy white woman."

A warm breeze carried the smell of wet manure through the front window.

"How do you and Frenchy get along?"

"Oh, he turned into a pretty good guy once we got past the slavery thing."

"The what?"

"One night he drank too much and hit me pretty hard. I couldn't figure out what I'd done. The next day he apologized. He said it had to do with 200 years of slavery. I understand it I guess, the anger and all."

"Aren't you afraid he'll do it again?"

"Oh, no. It was just the one time. See all those orange trees out there in the backyard? He planted every one of them. And he's going to dig a hole for a swimming pool too."

"Are you sure about all this?" I gulped down the rest of my drink.

"I know it's a little freaky, and some days I don't know how to handle it. Thank God for weed. I've made my bed, as they say. Besides, black men are better in that area."

"Bigger than white men?"

"And better kissers too. There's more cushion to their lips." Arlene pursed hers and made in and out motions like a fish.

*Maybe I should try it*, I thought. I didn't know if I could stand to be called a nigger lover. I thought that was a southern expression from another era. I'd have to live in a big city or someplace in Europe. But maybe if I loved the guy, I could live anywhere, including backward, conservative Phoenix.

"Are you in love with him?"

"I wish I'd had the chance to find out for sure before I got pregnant. If you want to try it out, I could introduce you to Frenchy's cousin. He's cute. You look good though. This guy Ray must be treating you right."

"I guess. He's a lot older. Can I try on your Afro?"

"It's cool, huh?" Arlene pulled off the wig. Her hair was bleached platinum underneath. In her short, African-print tunic with almond-shaped brown beads around her neck, she looked heavier without the big hair to give her more height.

I went down the hall to the bathroom to look in the mirror. Arlene turned up the sound on the television. In the darkness of the hallway, I could barely see the wall photos of Arlene's parents, her brother and the portrait I'd painted of her in high school: thin, tan, blonde, smiling and in love with Jerry, the guy she wanted to marry.

The walls of the bathroom were painted forest green. The color of the shag rug and toilet seat cover matched.

The light was low. I almost didn't see the baby lizard making its way across the windowsill.

I looked at myself in the mirror and then made my way back to the kitchen. "It's good with my skin color. Exotic, don't you think? Like I'm part Brazilian, black, and Irish or something."

Arlene twirled around on her barstool to face me. "Far out," she said. "It's great. Frenchy'll dig it."

"Where'd you meet him?"

"That place we used to go for burgers when we ditched school. The Ranch House. He was on a job nearby and stopped to eat his lunch out back at those picnic tables. He had on really tight bellbottoms." Arlene wiggled her hips on the bar stool and smacked her lips. "He knows how to give that good lovin' every night. Anyway, he politely asked if he could join me. Frenchy makes good money too as long as the construction jobs keep coming in. In the summer he has to eat salt tablets it gets so hot. One hundred twenty degrees some days. He never complains. He's used to hard times. When he was a kid in Greenwood, Mississippi, he and his brother used to walk to school through the rain in their mother's high heels. Isn't that a trip? They didn't have shoes of their own."

"Your mother must be thrilled about all this."

"You can imagine. She did loan me the money to buy the ring."

We watched silently as the soap opera ended.

"Are you still painting?" Arlene asked.

"Yeah. Ray said I could turn his garage into a studio."

"That's great. Listen, I'm going to have Ollie baptized and I wanted to know if you'd be his godmother. If I die, you need to make sure he gets Catholic teachings."

"Why me? I haven't seen you in years. And I'm not Catholic."

"I know we drifted apart, probably my fault, but we go back a long way."

She hadn't said that before. Maybe she had changed. I nodded and took a deep breath.

"I told Father Michael you were brought up Episcopalian. He said that was close enough for a godmother. You have to promise you'd make sure he got Catholic teachings."

Arlene went to the kitchen to warm a bottle. "Do you want to see him now? I have to warn you, he's pretty dark."

We went to the baby's room. It was the same color as the bathroom except one wall was covered with bamboo print wallpaper, ripped at the seams. Sunlight seeped in from the edges of an ill-fitting window shade pulled down below the windowsill. One stuffed teddy bear sat on a shelf above Ollie's crib.

"See what I mean?"

She hadn't exaggerated his darkness. It was hard to believe he'd come out of her.

"Well, he's a pretty color," I said. "Shiny burned umber."

"What's that?"

"A dark reddish-brown."

He was a skinny baby. He lay in the middle of a small mattress covered with an animal print sheet. His body was like a wooden board. Arlene didn't pick him up. She put the bottle in a plastic holder next to him. Ollie turned his tiny head. His eyes stared up at me as he sucked at the fake nipple.

We heard Frenchy come through the garage door singing.

"Hey, Arlene, you here?"

We went to the kitchen to meet him. His hair was cut short against his head. His jeans hung low on his hips. When he pulled off his white T-shirt and tossed it on the counter, he exposed his flat-muscled belly. His navel was encircled with an oval of black curly hair. He opened the refrigerator and bent down to get a beer.

"Where have you been?" asked Arlene.

"Hey, baby." Frenchy put his arm around her. "Out to the Junkanoo Club talking with Marvin. We came up with a dynamite idea. We're going into business together."

Arlene looked at me and rolled her eyes.

"Who's your friend?"

"This is Linda."

"Oh, the artist. Nice to meet you." Frenchy extended his hand toward me.

"We're gonna manufacture Marvin's Deep Pit Barbecue Sauce."

He had a thick southern accent. I had to listen closely to understand what he said.

"White people in this town aren't going to buy barbecue sauce from a couple of brothers," Arlene said.

"Sure they will. We'll be like Famous Amos, advertise our own thing. Start on local TV. We'll film Marvin digging a pit, then slapping sauce all over a pig and lowering it down into the ground. You girls can eat the finished product on camera."

"Nobody roasts pigs in pits anymore, except in Hawaii."

"Baby, it's just advertising."

"What do you think of my idea?" he said to me.

I paused to make sure I understood him. "Sounds good. Everyone should go for what they believe in."

"I am wore out. That is the bad part about all this. You

get a house and you got to work harder. I'm too young for this." Frenchy laughed.

"Did you bring the diapers?"

"Aw, shit." Frenchy shrugged his shoulders and slid his hands into the back pockets of his jeans. "Sorry, babe. I'll go now."

"Never mind. Give me the keys? Come on, Linda."

"Let her stay. I can show her the wall out back where you thought she could paint pink flamingos."

I looked at Arlene, then at Frenchy. He scared me a little but I was curious about him. Besides the fact that he was black, he seemed different from other men I'd met.

Arlene shot Frenchy a look of warning, raising her eyebrows and cocking her head. Had he cheated on her?

"Oh, all right. I'll be back in a few," she said.

Frenchy angled the blinds until the bands of light on the faded linoleum floor disappeared. "Have to keep the heat out," he said smiling. "So, Linda. What's happening?"

"Nothing much." My voice was higher than usual. My fingers tingled. I crossed my arms and held them tight.

"Let me get you another margarita." He went to the kitchen, pulled his shirt over his torso, and pulsed the blender. "Did you see my main man in there?"

"He's real cute. Looks like you."

"Cigarette? There on the table. They're made for black folk."

I noticed the brand. Parliaments.

"You smoke it, you might turn."

I laughed nervously. "No, thanks."

"That Afro looks good on you."

"Oh, I forgot all about it." I felt my face flush. I should have taken it off, but now my own hair would be a matted-down mess underneath. I smoothed the fake hair with my hand like it was my own.

"Let's sit down." He put my drink and his beer on the coffee table and patted the couch cushion. I sat in the chair across from him. "You did that painting of John Coltrane Arlene's got hanging in the bedroom. I like it. We'll go out back in a minute. Flamingos look good with a pool. Don't you think?"

"Sure," I said. *A picture he must have seen in a magazine*, I thought.

"I don't expect you to paint them for free or nothing. I used to draw as a kid. I drew things I wanted, like people going out to dinner. I got good at drawing cheeseburgers, tomatoes, onions, cheese, and secret sauce dripping over the side of a bun." Frenchy guzzled down half his beer. "My folks never took me anywhere when I was a kid. I mean nowhere. I've never even been on an airplane. I made paper ones all the time. My old man said, 'You doing something girls do.' He thought I was cutting out paper dolls. Can you believe it?" Frenchy leaned toward me with big eyes. "I tried to tell him, 'No. They fly.' But he wouldn't listen."

"How'd you end up in Arizona?"

"After my sister moved to Phoenix, my brother and I left Mississippi for good and drove out here. I was nineteen. Arlene said you used to write poetry."

"Yeah. Real depressing, suicidal stuff."

"Can I read you one of mine? You'll dig it. Wait here."

He went down the hall and came back carrying a red notebook. He flipped through a pile of records and put one on the turntable. "Background music. This poem is from a dream. Two dreams put together. Ready?" He turned some pages, stopping somewhere in the middle of the notebook. "I call this one 'The Nagi Man.'" His body began to sway to the reggae music.

*The Nagi man takes you down*
*Behind the shadow wall*
*Hey, baby, come with me*
*It's time for ecstasy*
*Oya sings below the tracks*
*Magnolia in her hair*
*Black arms wait to hold you*
*No more twists of fear*

Before I could say anything, he explained that in African mythology, Oya was a black goddess with nine heads, the queen of the winds of change. "When she opens her mouth, flicks out her tongue," he said, imitating Oya, "lightning strikes."

As he talked, I pictured myself in Arlene's shoes. I couldn't raise a black child in Phoenix any better than she. I couldn't handle the gawking and whispering, but I saw why she'd been attracted to Frenchy. He was real, sensual, and spontaneous.

The margaritas began to make my head buzz. The edges of my body felt doughy and thick.

"You got a man, Linda?"

"I live with him in Hollywood. People keep asking me when I'm going to settle down."

"If this guy's not the one, don't settle. You look good. You got style, and you got talent too."

He turned up the music, took my hand, and pulled me up from the couch. I hesitated but then followed his lead to the rhythm of the reggae. He held me close. I tried to imitate his hip movements. I wanted to taste the salt on his skin. Dancing with Frenchy to the music of Bob Marley was a far cry from sitting around with Ray listening to Patti Page sing "The Folks Who Live on the Hill." Sometimes with Ray I felt sucked into childhood, remembering the music my mother listened to through all her marriages and divorces.

Ollie began to cry.

"I'll get him," I said.

Still moving to the music, I came back to the den holding Ollie's stiff body in my arms. His skin was moist. He smiled.

"He knows I'm going to be his godmother," I said.

"That's my man." Frenchy moved closer to me. His bare arm touched mine. He stroked the baby's face. Ollie laughed, and for a moment our skin stuck together.

I looked out the back window as the afternoon sun shot streaks of yellow light into the leaves of the orange trees. I heard the cranking cogwheel sound of the garage door opening.

Frenchy moved away from me. Arlene came in with a box of diapers.

"Hey," she said, sizing us up. "I ran into Marcus at the store. He's having a barbeque right now. He invited us over for a burger."

"How about it Linda, we can all go?" Frenchy said.

"Sure."

"I don't want to take Ollie. Linda can stay here with him; get to know her godson. We won't be gone long."

I handed her the baby.

"What?"

"I have to go."

"Why?"

"What about the flamingos?" said Frenchy.

"Paint them yourself."

"What's with you?" Arlene said.

On my way out, I held my breath as I walked by the freshly manured front lawn.

# Teeth and Eyes, Girls!

One by one they arrived at the Sunburst Hotel, the names of their cities sashed across their bodies in red letters embossed on white satin. Miss Gila Bend; Miss Yuma; Miss Kingman; Miss Glendale; Miss Prescott; Miss Tempe; Miss Bisbee; Miss Nogales; Miss Fort Apache; Miss Tucson; Miss Carefree, Miss Casa Grande; Miss Wickenburg; Miss Flagstaff; Miss Tombstone; Miss Winslow, from the Navajo tribe; and Miss Mesa, a black girl. Until a year ago, girls of color were not allowed to enter the Miss Arizona pageant.

The real beauties were Miss Mesa, who had no chance of winning, (there wouldn't be a black Miss Arizona until 1995) and Miss Carefree, rumored to hold many pageant titles in California. She looked like a pro with her slim body and perfectly coiffed, shoulder-length, blonde hair. Her smile didn't slip for a moment.

My mother, a former fashion model, had tried for years to get me to smile like that. When I was five, she trained me to walk poolside runways at the Wigwam and Westward Ho resorts in Phoenix. I was good at pivoting, but shy about smiling for strangers.

"I don't understand how you got that way," she said. "You couldn't have inherited it from me."

Before we walked onto the runway, she put Vaseline on my gums so my lips would slide back easily when I smiled.

"What if I don't feel like smiling?" I said.

"It doesn't matter. You have to kill them with friendliness."

"But it's a lie."

"They don't know the difference, honey. Make them believe you're having more fun than you've ever had in your whole life. Hold your head up and don't squint, even if the sun is in your eyes."

I never got the hang of it.

No matter what, my mother believed that style and charm could mask anything, including three failed marriages, an inheritance stolen by an ex-husband, and a swift descent from a life of privilege to a low-rent studio apartment with a brown lawn and no trees, not even a cactus.

Since my mother had trained me so well to notice limitations, I tried not to be judgmental as I watched the other contestants come through the front door of the hotel. Most of the girls were unattractive by beauty queen standards and walked with their legs too far apart, a cardinal sin according to my mother. Although I looked the part, I'd always balked when, over the years, people said I should be a model, an actress, a talk show host, or a newscaster. But I wanted to be an artist. I'd sold some drawings and paintings, and I had three pieces hanging in a gallery, but sales were spotty.

Ray supported me so I could paint, but he wanted a wife and kids. I couldn't live up to the bargain. I wanted to go to art school.

I left him and L.A., moved back to Phoenix, and went to work at Mabel Murphy's, a new western-themed bar with a hitching post outside the front door. I didn't have experience as a bartender, and I had no desire to become one, but the manager said the tips were substantial. I had to wear a cowgirl costume: a purple polyester shirt with snaps and ruffles down the front, a fake suede miniskirt with fringe, and a cheap, silver-studded cowboy hat.

After a few weeks of training, I could memorize twenty drinks at a time as the cocktail waitresses rattled them off. I felt a fleeting sense of accomplishment and tried to cheer myself up by approaching the job as if it were a temporary novelty act.

One night, my mother came into Mabel Murphy's with her husband, Carl, the industrial laundry machine salesman. He'd come onto me one day after describing in detail his sex life with my mother while we were having a lunch to discuss what gifts he should give her for Christmas. I threw all the tableware across the room and walked out.

After three vodka gimlets, my mother put her head down and wept. When she came up for air, she said, "How did it come to this, you here mixing drinks? You should have stayed with Ray."

My fantasy that the job was just a temporary diversion went down the drain with my mother's tears and customers' undrunk margaritas and beer. Who was I kidding? Bartending could be it for the rest of my life.

A week later, as I set up the bar for the evening, a tall, attractive blond guy, too well dressed to be from Phoenix, sat down and ordered a martini. He stared at me while I made it.

"Olives?" I said.

"Two. Do I know you?"

"I don't think so." I shook his martini, poured it in a glass, and set it in front of him.

He took a sip, and I noticed a gold and ruby ring on his right little finger that looked familiar.

"Perfect," he said. "Is your name Linda?"

"Yes, it is. Why?"

"I'm Arlene's brother, David. Remember me?"

"David? I haven't seen you since you were in seventh grade." He'd been an annoying twelve-year-old who chased us with jars of bees and threatened to open the lids.

He stood up, leaned across the bar, and hugged me.

"It's so good to see you," he said, sitting back down.

I took a deep breath, staring at his hands. "You too. Your ring, didn't that belong to your father?"

"Yeah. He died a couple years ago."

"I'm sorry." I wondered if David had forgiven him for leaving his mom.

"You look great."

"In this getup?" I said. "Thanks." I walked to the end of the bar and started wiping it down. "This is the easiest task of bartending. Being approachable, knowledgeable, entertaining, making even difficult people comfortable, all while making perfect drinks is exhausting. What have you been you up to all these years?"

"I live in New York now, studying musical theatre. I'm here visiting my mom."

"Oh, right, you used to listen to Broadway show tunes and sing along. Really loud. "

He laughed. "Oh, sorry about that."

"How do you like New York?" I sliced lemons and limes into twists, spirals, wedges, and wheels.

"I love it. I've performed in lots of musical theatre productions in New Jersey." He held up crossed fingers. "One day, Broadway."

*Gay*, I thought. "How's your mother?"

"She's good. She loves it when I'm in town and can choose her outfits."

*Definitely, gay.*

"Are you still painting?"

"Not as much as I'd like. I don't have much energy after this, and the tips aren't as good as I thought they'd be. I wish I had money for art school. Painting is the only thing that keeps me sane."

"You definitely should. Have you seen Arlene?"

"We're not in touch anymore."

"Me either."

Two guys in cowboy hats came in and sat down at the far end of the bar. "Hey, little lady, how about a couple beers, whatever you got on tap." I served them with a failed smile and went back to talk to David.

"You know, if you want more money, you should enter the Miss Arizona pageant. I saw an article about it in the paper."

"I could never do anything like that."

"Why not? You could win a scholarship. It might lead to something."

"You met my mother, right? I don't want to be like her."

"You're not. Do the pageant."

He wrote his number on a cocktail napkin. "Call me. I'd love to stay in touch."

\*\*\*

The late afternoon sun shot through cracks in the lobby's vertical blinds. I sat under a ten-foot palm tree in a

Mexican pigskin chair, wearing the Miss Phoenix sash, waiting for whoever my roommate would be and our chaperone, wondering if I'd made a mistake. What had seemed a harmless way to win money or a scholarship, a joke really, now felt suffocating, like a lockdown in a beauty prison with my mother as the warden. I imagined the judges were already watching, giving me poor marks for not chit-chatting with the other girls.

My original title had been Miss Cave Creek. I applied late to the contest and all the other towns were taken. Cave Creek wasn't a town, but a big piece of desert with a gas station barely visible from the highway. I had to choose a costume that would represent my city. Wearing a green leotard and tights painted with stripes and prickly needles with yellow flowers attached to the top of my head would represent all the blooming barrel cacti in Cave Creek. The director, Miss Litchfield Park 1943, thought I was joking. "The pageant is a serious event. Please choose something appropriate."

I didn't have to. Two weeks before the contest began, the judges discovered an "unsavory detail" in Miss Phoenix's past. They wouldn't disclose it, but they disqualified her and offered me the title. "You look like a representation of the capital," they said. I didn't consider this a compliment. I'd always thought of Phoenix as a hick town. The judges told me to wear a tennis costume since so many tennis stars played in Phoenix and had homes there. How boring.

I didn't know how to sing or play an instrument or twirl batons. I only knew how to draw and paint, so I was relieved to learn that this particular Miss Arizona contest, sponsored by Miss USA, did not require a talent.

Before I could officially compete, I needed a sponsor to

pay for registration fees, hotel expenses, and my wardrobe. My mother, thrilled I'd finally made a good life decision, took me to see her friend, Louie Germain, owner of Chez Louie, the first and only French restaurant in Scottsdale. Women were crazy for his hand kissing, French talking, and good food.

"So tall. Such beauty. *Bonne publicitè*," he said and agreed to sponsor me. The pressure began. Louie put my picture in the menu as if I were an entrée, along with an announcement about the pageant.

I agonized over the thought of parading around in a bathing suit. I knew that bright overhead lights, like the noonday sun, would accentuate every puckered fat cell. I spent every day before the competition not eating much and exercising on all the machines at the new Jack LaLanne health club. My low back ached from the tightening, but I kept up the routine until my flesh turned harder and jiggled less.

\*\*\*

An hour later, my roommate, Miss Tucson, found me still sitting in the pigskin chair under the palm tree in the lobby. Extremely thin, with an even thinner ponytail, she introduced herself. "I don't know what I'm doing here," she said. "I've never even curled my hair."

"Why'd you come?"

"My parents want me to win the scholarship money. I was picked from ten other girls at my riding stable. My name is Stacey, by the way."

"I'm Linda. I'm here for scholarship money too."

Our chaperone, Joan, came over to meet us. "We need to check in right away," she said. When she walked, her pantyhose made a swishing sound as her thick piano legs rubbed against each other.

As soon as we got to our room, Joan, a retired seamstress who'd made custom debutante and bridal gowns for wealthy Arizona girls, showed Stacey how to put rollers in her hair. She told us that before the five finalists were chosen, we would be judged on everything: appearance in bathing suits and evening gowns, interactions with others, and table manners.

"The judges will watch you eat," she said.

To impress them, I decided I wouldn't change my fork back to my right hand after cutting something, like I'd seen in foreign films. It looked more sophisticated and made more sense than the American way.

"I'll be staying in the connecting room next door," Joan said. "Starting now, you can't have any contact with the outside."

"Can I make one last phone call?" I asked.

She agreed. I called David, told him I'd entered the pageant, and invited him to the events.

"You're on your way!" he said. *To what?* But maybe he was right; this would lead to something beyond Mabel Murphy's.

\*\*\*

Joan gave Stacey and me diet pills when we started to fade during the fourteen-hour days of the competition. Before menopause, my mother took diet pills for PMS. She said they lightened her mood before her period. I never noticed a difference. One day when I was younger, and she was having a particularly intense bout of pre-menstrual hell, I told her a boy at school had come up to me and said, "You're pretty." Her response: "I've never thought you were that pretty." Shocked by the punch to my stomach, I decided from then on to keep compliments to myself and try my best to believe them.

In the Roadrunner Ballroom, we practiced what I'd already learned as a child: how to smile with the help of petroleum jelly. And how to step, place, and pivot at the end of a runway. I expected to hear backbiting, and maybe it would come later, but most girls were only eighteen, away from their small towns for the first time, and too inexperienced to know how to be malicious. I could tell Miss Carefree knew but didn't bother; she had no competition in this group.

We had ten-minute individual interviews with the five judges—three ex-beauty queens and two men. I didn't mention bartending. I talked about art and wanting to go to school. Saturday night we competed in evening gowns for an audience on a makeshift runway, and the next night in orange Catalina one-piece swimsuits.

David came backstage after the swimsuit competition and surprised me with a huge bouquet of summer flowers. I hadn't seen him or Louie, my sponsor, in the audience, only my mother, sitting straighter than anyone else, smiling big, and pointing at her mouth.

David hugged me. He smelled of sage and lavender. I wanted to move closer to him, as if he was a forgotten twin who'd been lost and now found.

"I've never seen anyone project so much energy on stage," he said. "You belong in New York."

"I'm not serious about this, you know."

"You have something special." He ran his hand through his thick wavy hair.

"Who's this? Your brother?" said Joan.

"Yes."

"No outsiders, even if they are relatives. Let's go. We don't want to be disqualified."

*We? Did she get a prize if one of her girls won?*

David called out, "Come to New York with me."

I turned to wave goodbye and saw my mother coming toward me. I took Joan's arm, and we rushed away.

Back in our room, Joan gave Stacey and me wine so we could sleep. The next day she told me that I'd been chosen as one of five finalists. The local TV station would broadcast the final segment of the pageant, and the winner would be chosen. All the girls would wear their city costumes.

"This is so thrilling. It's the first time one of my girls has made it this far. But you don't seem very excited," she said.

"Oh, but I am."

I felt panic. If I won, I'd be obligated to go on to the Miss USA pageant. Given my background, would I become completely beauty brainwashed? Would I still care about a scholarship?

Stacey hugged me and said, "Congratulations," but when she pulled away, she hung her head and her newfound curls covered her face. At dinner that night, the other girls acted happy for me, but I saw a few of them, including Miss Carefree, whispering to each other when they thought I wasn't looking.

Before the TV show, Joan shortened my tennis skirt—"More leg doesn't hurt," she said—and suggested I wear my hair in pigtails tied with ribbons to offset the sexier skirt with cuteness.

"Do you win something if I win?" I asked.

"I can't discuss that."

At the rehearsal, the director shouted over and over, "When we go live, give me teeth and eyes, girls, teeth and eyes." He told us to shriek with happiness when the new Miss Arizona was named, huddle around her with hugs and kisses. "Everyone on board?" All the girls clapped, and I followed suit.

The last part of the competition was hosted by Pat McMahon, a local guy who played the characters Aunt Maud, a senior citizen, and Gerald, the most hated kid in America, on the "Wallace and Ladmo" children's show, which I had found stupid by age four.

I gripped the handle of my tennis racket when it was my turn to answer the judges' questions.

"So Linda," said Pat, referring to the stack of cards he held, "the judges want to know what you want to do in life."

"I'm an artist."

"And who is your favorite artist?"

"Chagall."

His face went blank. "Cha who?" he said, looking around with his hands in the air, laughing. The audience snickered.

"He's famous," I said. But Pat moved on to Miss Carefree and asked her more questions than he asked me.

When she was named the winner—no surprise—I thought I had huddled and hugged like the other girls, but later when I saw a tape of the show, I was surprised to see myself standing slightly off to the side with a snide look.

"Your bosom didn't look good in that swimsuit," my mother said. She also told me I didn't win because of my down-turned mouth.

Two days after the pageant, a place called Destiny Unlimited offered to train me as a professional beauty queen. The director, a former beauty queen from Mississippi and one of the judges assessed me in a southern voice: "Honey, your hair needs to be strawberry blonde. You have to learn to smile as if you mean it. And sweetie, the way you use your silverware isn't American. You act too sophisticated. You spoke Spanish to the busboys."

"All I said was '*Gracias.*'"

When I met with her, she handed me a *Pageant Prep* manual. "You have the raw material to be a star. Look through this and let me know if you want to talk about signing a contract."

I didn't tell my mother. I called David.

"You looked beautiful on TV. You should have won," he said.

"I was terrified I would. I wasn't very friendly."

"You were very perky during the question part until that guy started laughing. So you weren't Miss Apple Pie. Boring. You stood out from the crowd. That's what counts in New York. Forget this beauty queen stuff. You're better than that."

"You should see this prep manual. It reads like that book, *The Stepford Wives.*"

\*\*\*

David and I went to the Phoenix Ballet's performance of *Swan Lake* and made fun of how clumsy and thick-waisted the dancers were. He pointed out how they'd been improperly trained. "What can you expect from this cow town?"

David's musical theatre optimism cheered me up. He played Broadway show tunes, mostly *Pippin*, and sang along in his high, crystalline voice. He took me to dance classes in mom-and-pop studios filled with teenage girls, their mothers watching from the sidelines. David's legs seemed to grow longer as he leapt across a dance floor. He'd studied with the Joffrey Ballet. I re-discovered my natural talent from childhood ballet lessons. We danced until two in the morning at the Red Dog Club in Scottsdale. People cleared the floor to watch us.

We cruised around town acting snotty and dramatic, shocking people with our outfits. My favorites: a strapless lobster print dress hand-beaded by David, four inch platform sandals, and a large straw hat trimmed with red berries; and him in loose, white summer linen, looking like F. Scott Fitzgerald. Most people in Phoenix wore ill-fitting shorts, flip-flops, and had badly permed hair.

David gave me red roses and a hand-painted scarf of a Chagall painting for my birthday.

I went back to work at the bar until I saved 500 bucks and money for plane fare. One night, David and I were drunk and we decided I should cut my waist-length hair in a female version of his, a style he saw in *Vogue* magazine.

The hairdresser, a friend of David's, brushed all my hair into a ponytail and asked if I was ready. My eyes welled up. I gripped the arms of the chair. David squeezed my hand. I started to perspire under the black nylon cape, smelling bleach, dye, and shampoo wafting through the salon. Then he cut—more like sawed through—my thick ponytail. My head and neck began to move more easily. I took a deep breath.

"Thank God," said David. "Goodbye Apple Pie. Hello Big Apple."

When I told my mother I was moving to New York, she said, "With that haircut, be sure to wear plenty of make-up or people will think you're a dyke."

David bought me a pair of fake green and gold snakeskin

platforms. He thought I should be performing. Maybe he was right. I was still a good dancer.

Before we left Phoenix, I did a painting called "I Think I'll Move to New York"—a blue-black desert floor leading to a tiny window framed in purple, a vast pale blue sky beyond.

# Mr. Fairy Dust

In August, I moved from Arizona into David's roach-infested brownstone studio apartment on West 75th between Broadway and Columbus, owned by Miss Daisy Mills (she insisted we call her by her full name), a widow in her seventies who hadn't left the house in ten years except to sit on her front stoop and chain smoke the unfiltered Pall Malls that David brought her from the corner newsstand every day.

From our third-floor, small, concrete slab of a balcony, I could see rooms in other buildings, upside down mops leaning in corners, ravaged plants, and clotheslines full of laundry strung across the empty space between one brownstone and another. When the temperature reached ninety degrees and stayed there through the night, David and I climbed out the window to the balcony to suck in thick, stinky air before going to sleep in the double sofa bed he'd found on the street. He said when the weather turned cold, the bed bugs would stop biting.

One day, I wandered through the city comparing it to the vastness of the Arizona desert and the white-bread Phoenix neighborhood where I'd grown up. I took in the buildings, the storefronts, the cars, yellow cabs, and the

people: mixtures of style, age, and color, alive and ener-
getic, all rushing to get somewhere. I wanted to absorb
everything. I stood for a while at the edge of Central Park
West in my six-inch platform shoes and eyelash-length
hair, breathing in the smells of the city. For the first time
in my life, I didn't feel like a freak.

I hadn't calculated how much money I'd need to get
settled in New York. The 500 I'd saved from my bartending
job in Scottsdale disappeared after I paid my half of the
rent and, at David's insistence, bought a series of dance
classes at the Alvin Ailey studio. He wanted to guide my
musical theatre career. I hadn't yet seen a Broadway show,
but David suggested I go to a dance audition for *Gypsy*,
for a non-union theatre in New Jersey.

"Act real sexy," he said.

I did, and they gave me a part.

"I told you, you have theatrical potential. Just call me
Mr. Fairy Dust."

I turned down the role. There was no pay. I had to
work. David introduced me to Diane, his agent at the
Career Blazers Temp Agency, who sent him on jobs to
clean apartments, walk dogs, and serve at private parties.
She was impressed with my typing speed and said she
could give me office and other kinds of work. With my
bartending experience, I'd imagined myself making a
fortune in tips, mixing drinks in The Oak Room at The
Plaza, wearing something more dignified than the cowgirl
costume I'd had to wear at Mabel Murphy's bar, and
meeting people with clout, but I discovered there were
no women bartenders in Manhattan in 1973. I'd expected
New York to be ahead of Arizona.

Diane sent me to Tony Bennett's home to serve drinks
for a family birthday party. At the end of the evening,

Tony's wife didn't give me a tip, but he slipped me a twenty before I left.

My job as a roving hostess for Brew Burger restaurants lasted two weeks. I worked at a different franchise every day, from the slummy West Side to the chichi East Side, made minimum wage—two dollars an hour—and no tips. I could have a meal, a burger and fries, but no beer. To overcome boredom, I gave Tarot card readings to the customers and was fired.

Diane sent me to entertain at a children's birthday party. I told her I had no experience with children. "You'll think of something," she said. I dressed as Raggedy Ann and did a loose-limbed doll dance. They laughed, but when a boy asked me why Andy hadn't come, I couldn't think of anything to say except he'd had an accident. The kids cried. "He's fine. He's fine," I said. The tears stopped when I told them he would visit soon, and they could sign the cast on his arm.

I typed, filed, and answered phones all over the city. Some offices still had rickety old typewriters, no knowledge of an IBM Selectric or Wite-Out. At one job, I asked the man in charge, who wore two sweaters dotted with small moth holes, about an eraser. He shook his long head and frowned.

Diane arranged an interview for me to teach ballroom dancing at the Fred Astaire Dance Studio. Except for vague memories of the waltz and foxtrot I had learned at Junior Dance Assembly in seventh grade, I didn't know any ballroom dances. "We'll train you eventually," the manager said, "but the way you look, all you have to know is how to give an introductory lesson and make sure the men think they're leading you."

"How do I do that?"

"We'll show you. It's a matter of giving them subtle signals with your hands. They feel like they're in charge, and the more body contact you give them, the more lessons you'll sell."

After a few weeks, tired of being groped by strange, lonely men, I quit. To cheer myself up, I went to Bergdorf Goodman's, opened a charge account, and bought a pair of 300 dollar sky-blue, rhinestone-studded, high-heeled suede boots. I wore them that night when David and I, in matching vintage fox fur jackets, made our usual rounds of the disco clubs. No one could tell pieces of fur had rotted or been worn away. David designed and sewed clothes for me, and we spent hours coordinating our outfits.

Sometimes, Diane sent David and me to work a party together, dressed like androgynous twins. We were six feet tall, had the same lean, long body and short, dark-blond hair. We spun around each other, bumped hips and shoulders while humming "Dancing Machine," as we served drinks, never spilling a drop.

We'd come home and after killing a few cockroaches, David would heat up pizza slices or make potatoes in a variety of ways.

"Your choice, madam," he'd say. "Roasted, scalloped, baked, or your favorite, fried mashed balls?" We'd eat day-old French pastries for dessert before opening up the pull-out sofa and falling into bed exhausted.

I hadn't expected to work so hard to get by. I was bone tired from the drudgery of boring nine-to-five jobs, taking dancing and singing lessons at night, dragging myself around the city, taking wrong subways and buses. I didn't know how to read a map. I took to walking long distances in high heels and tiptoeing over subway grates.

When the weather cooled, the bed bugs stopped biting,

but when it snowed several inches, I couldn't believe I had to walk through it. I'd never lived in snow and didn't have proper footwear. I had high heels, fake snake skin platforms, and clogs, which is what I wore with two pairs of socks and David's beat up ankle-length wool coat. He walked with me to the subway or bus stop and held my arm so I wouldn't stumble.

The other thing I hadn't expected was to fall in love with David. For my birthday, he gave me a bouquet of red roses, a 1940s beaded sweater, a hand-painted scarf, earrings, and chocolates. Most former boyfriends had been inattentive in comparison. I'd take them shopping, point out a specific item, easy things like perfume or costume jewelry, and say, "I'd like that for my birthday." Instead, they'd get me bath towels, a toaster oven, or something equally unromantic.

For Christmas, David made triple chocolate biscotti and surprised me with an art deco comb and brush set and an ivory-handled beveled mirror that I'd spotted in a store window months before, and for Valentine's Day, a hand-made, black-laced, heart-shaped card.

His constant gift giving and greeting card declarations of love confused me. But when he took me to a New Year's Eve party on a gay boat cruise around the Hudson, and I saw men sucking each other's cocks in the middle of the dance floor while David watched, smiling, mesmerized by the scene and the Pointer Sisters' "I'm So Excited," I knew I'd have to accept celibate love.

After the cruise, I felt as foolish as I had as a teenager the day my mother told me the sexy male models I swooned over in her *Vogue* magazines were gay.

David met a Buddhist who told him he should follow

Tina Turner's lead and start chanting Nam-myoho-renge-kyo for acting jobs and money. We made an altar with a dish of water, a green leaf, and a picture of a Buddhist monk on top of a file cabinet David had found on the street. One of the leaders blessed the altar and our entire apartment. Once a week during a big chanting meeting at the Church of Religious Science, people gave testimonials about how the more they chanted, the more they got what they wanted: houses, lovers, cars, jobs.

In the early morning before David woke, I quietly chanted for him to turn straight. The leader had said, "Anything and everything can happen, especially in New York."

My body continued to crave David's. I liked lying beside him at night and waking up next to him. I fantasized about his hands stroking my body, and guiding him inside me. Had he ever been with a woman? Before we left Arizona, David's Italian mother, who prayed for straightness or at least a grandchild from her son, took me aside and said, "He's very well-hung. See what you can do. You won't be disappointed." She lifted her eyebrows up and down like Groucho Marx and made a fucking gesture with her hands.

One night, David came home late from a bar. I lay still, waiting for him to fall asleep. His sweet, woody smell mixed with smoke, cheap pine cologne, and gin excited me. So did the thought of David with a strange-smelling man. I wanted to prove that sex with me could be better. I let my hand drift to the edge of his lanky thigh, stroked the length of his taut muscles. Maybe now was the time to take his mother's advice. David stirred, whispered my name, and turned away. I touched myself instead, silently giving in to my desire.

I thought of the woman I met in a dance class, in love with a gay man who told me she got so frustrated one night she forced herself on him. He rejected her in a hurtful way, and she never saw him again. She lost her best friend.

The next morning, David told me he'd had a vision in the bar. "A message from the grave," he said. He sat on the window ledge by the heater with his legs crossed. His free foot trembled from a tense ankle. Snow collected on the fire escape. "From my dead grandmother. I saw her face in the mirror behind the bar. There was a white mist around her head."

I brought David a cup of coffee. "Then what?"

"I heard her voice. I feel crazy telling you this."

"What did she say?"

He turned toward the snow-framed window. The heater hissed. "She said you and I were supposed to be together. Together—for life."

My skin began to tingle. A message from the grave held potential for a conversion. "What do you think?" I asked.

"I think she's right. You know I love you, but ..." David turned toward me, his eyes brimming with tears. "Maybe I could ... I never ... I don't know."

For a while, I initiated lengthy conversations about how and when David and I might take the sexual leap. He would definitely have to be drunk. He was afraid I'd make fun of him. I imagined that he'd be disgusted by me. I started to feel like a beggar.

I decided to pray to Grandma.

Out of desperation and rejection, and with no money for a therapist, I walked into St. Monica's, the neighborhood Catholic Church, and asked to see a priest. I wasn't Catholic, and I wasn't sure I believed in God, but David did. Father Jim was Irish, about fifty, and the hair on his balding head looked greasy. White flecks had scattered and stuck in the creases of his robe. The Virgin Mary in cut glass glowed with sunlight above his desk. He sat across from me, his stubby hands folded over his belly, and asked me to tell him about my family and David's. He said it sounded like David wasn't so much gay as afraid of intimacy. I had been hoping he'd say something like that, but I knew it wasn't true.

"If he'll come for counseling," he said, "there might be a chance for the two of you. If he won't, ask yourself why you've chosen an unavailable man."

David wouldn't talk to a priest. I decided to take Father Jim's advice and told David I had to move out.

"Where will you go?"

"I'll call my cousin."

"What about our act?"

We'd been scraping money together, taking voice lessons, learning to harmonize so we could create a song and dance act. Our vocal coach, Louis, had encouraged us and suggested that in between songs we give each other little kisses on stage. I'd looked forward to rehearsing that. We came up with "Davlin," for David and Linda, as the name for our act. I'd given him an ID bracelet with those letters on the front.

"I can't believe you're deserting me," he said. He paced around the apartment holding a little white bag from the bakery where he'd gone to get pastries.

I'd started to pack and hoped to be gone by the time he came back.

"It's not your fault, but I feel deserted every night," I said, folding my clothes into a black garbage bag. "I can't take the rejection."

"I'm not rejecting you. I love you."

"I need to feel desired. I don't want to be a thirty-year-old fag hag." I shoved David's creations of a beaded, lobster patterned dress and the silk eggshell one with a dropped waist and navy blue abstract flowers into the bag.

"You would never be that. I desire you, but it stops at a certain point. I want it to change," David said.

"It won't. You can't make it."

I wouldn't ever feel as close to any man as I did to David, but surely at some point he'd meet a guy he'd want to be with. Where would that leave me?

"You need to find a man, David."

"I know what we can do." He wrote something on a piece of paper. "Sign this. It's like a contract. If, at thirty-five, neither one of us is in a relationship, we can get together again and have a child."

"What?"

"Why not? You never know how things will go."

"You're crazy," I said. But the promise of a future of last resort, however unlikely, made it easier to let go, so I signed the paper.

I gathered my bags, then turned to see David sitting on the balcony, head down. As much as my body wanted him, I walked it out the door, dragging my belongings behind me.

# The Colonel,
# The Mogul,
# and Me

My cousin Jimmie said I could stay at his place until I could get my own apartment, so I moved into his one bedroom on 61st and Lexington that he shared with his much younger, South African girlfriend, Judy. Jimmie was my mother's first cousin and a few years older than she. He had additional homes in Fort Lauderdale, the Bahamas, and London. I hadn't seen him in ten years.

The living room was filled with African artifacts and animal skins, some I didn't recognize, spread out over the wood floors. He bragged about writing a book—the story of his world travels, his hunting trips, and the many women he'd slept with, including the Happy Hooker.

"I shot all these," he said, indicating the animals on the floor with a sweep of his hand.

When he left the room, I looked underneath the skins and found price tags.

I slept on the leather couch in the living room. When he and Judy came home late to entertain friends, I had to rise up from a deep sleep, pop up from under the blanket like a jack-in-the box, introduce myself, and make room for people to sit down. Occasionally, they took me out to dinner as a date for their out-of-town male business associates. In the mornings, they drank mimosas from crystal glasses and played backgammon for money.

I was too sleep deprived to keep up with full-time temp jobs. Now that I wasn't paying rent, I could work half as much.

I called David every few days to recount the distressing details of my new living situation in safari land. Each time we spoke, he'd say, "Please come back."

One night in my sleep, I slid off the leather couch and bumped my head on the glass coffee table. Mounted baby elephant tusks tumbled to their sides. When I opened my eyes, I saw Jimmie standing over me, naked, his angular body swaying from side to side as if he were doing some kind of dance on the zebra skin. His white hair gleamed in the dark. I thought it was my imagination or a dream. By the time I was fully awake, he was gone. Judy's angry voice soon came from the bedroom. He said, "Just a glass of water." I heard a slap and several minutes of muffled sounds, crying, and then silence. I stayed awake the rest of the night afraid the bedroom door would open again.

The next morning, Judy handed me a mimosa and asked me to leave. She said she didn't trust Jimmie around me.

"I haven't encouraged him. He's my cousin," I said. I knew that didn't mean anything.

"That's legal in some places. It's not you," said Judy. "He's been going out to the living room every night. We've been fighting about it."

"Every night?" My skin crawled.

\*\*\*

I was thirteen when, after the divorce from Jack, my mother, sister, and I moved to Fort Lauderdale because Jimmie had promised to help my mother out financially.

She told us he designed lobbies and restaurants for high-end hotels all over the world. He'd divorced his second wife, a Danish woman named Inge, because she went to bed too early and couldn't keep up with his jet-set lifestyle.

The day we arrived, he picked us up at the airport in a vintage Rolls Royce and took us to one of the restaurants he'd designed overlooking the water in Boca Raton. "Reservations for Colonel Renfrew," he said to the hostess. He didn't look like a colonel. He wore a blazer and closed shoes with no socks. While we waited to be seated, he sent us to the ladies room to check out the Italian tile he'd chosen for the floor and the walls.

He ordered oysters for us and lit a cigar. "Cuban," he said. He and my mother drank two bottles of white wine. She held her face in a forced smile until the alcohol took over and her mouth went slack.

"Gail, you'll love it here." He puffed and puffed. "Just love it. You can stay tan all year long, best place in the world besides the Bahamas."

"I can tell it's going to be marvelous fun," my mother said.

"Great place for young people. How old are you?" he asked me. I could see my mother in his jaw. I didn't answer.

He blew smoke in my direction.

"Where will we live?" my sister asked.

"I'll take care of that." He patted her head.

He talked funny. His mouth was like a clamp screwed down almost solid. It moved with a small dark space in between his lips.

He took us to a rental house on a canal owned by a friend of his. "You can live here for a great price." My mother had counted on something rent-free until she found a job, which she'd never had except for poolside modeling at high-end resorts in Phoenix.

We lived in the house for a month. She ran out of money, and we moved to a cheap apartment in Pompano Beach.

The Saturday Jimmie invited us to go snorkeling, Kimberly had a sore throat and my mother had a job interview for a salesgirl position at Saks Fifth Avenue.

"This is a good sign. It's a family event, and he's including us," my mother said. She hadn't given up hope. The outing would be a test of worthiness I'd have to face alone. So far, he'd only offered a vague invitation for a future visit to his home on Cat Island. But we needed money for food and rent.

I'd never been snorkeling or on a sailboat. My mother wanted me to look perfect, but she had no idea what that should be. She must have pictured herself lounging on a yacht sipping a drink with an umbrella straw and forgot that it was I who was actually going and that this was an athletic event. With her precious savings, she bought me my first bikini, thong sandals, and an inappropriate lace cover up to hide my sheltered white stomach. "You do good," she said. "And have fun."

When Jimmie came to pick me up, and I saw him and my third cousins, five towheaded, perfectly tanned aquatic experts dressed in their old tennis shoes and sweat shirts, I was sure they had no intention of including me in their boating rituals. I was off to a bad start—the newly poor, fatherless relative dressed for poolside.

I was determined to fit in, but I didn't do well with the snorkeling. I couldn't get the breathing right and had to come back on deck after a few minutes. Thin red slices on my stomach, arms and legs—cuts from the coral reef—

burned and stung once I was out of the water and into the ocean air. Jimmie came on deck and sprayed me with some kind of antiseptic.

"You're sunburned too," he said. "You need to get tanned up." His hands eased around to my stomach and his fingers edged up under my ruffled bikini top. He undid the clasp in the front. I looked down at his hands, like shelves, holding up my small breasts and then mashing them around in his big palms. I counted the number of bolts in the bottom of the boat until he finished.

"We'll have to get your mother and sister out here." He dove in and swam toward the five yellow breathing tubes bobbing in the ocean.

I gazed out at the water and focused on the glistening light wondering if this would make up for my inadequacies.

\*\*\*

"Not only is there a problem with Jim, you have way too many clothes taking up space in our closet. When can you leave?" said Judy.

Shafts of bright light fell through the cracked blinds and struck her face. She was a thin, dark-haired woman with downy hair on her upper lip. I remembered the day her girlfriend from South Africa had come to visit. I over-heard them in the kitchen whispering about how lucky Judy was to have hooked a rich chap like Jim and that abortions were finally legal in the states.

Her nervous, stick-like fingers opened the backgammon board. She began organizing the chips. I noticed her ravaged cuticles, the chewed-up fingernails, bitten down as if by tiny rats.

"Does he want me to leave?"

"Yes, he does."

This was confirmed when Jimmie appeared after his shower, wrapped in a towel with West Palm Beach monogrammed in turquoise letters across his hips, and said, "Did Judy talk to you?"

I'd hoped blood would run thick. The Colonel owed me. His strange nighttime behavior scared me, but I couldn't go back to David. I made myself another mimosa.

From then on, Judy hardly spoke to me, and they stopped fixing me up with dinner dates.

One night, John Rhar, a sixty-year-old British gold buyer, and his date, a young woman named Alexandra, came over for cocktails. Alexandra had no last name and spoke with a fake transcontinental accent.

Alex and I became friendly over the next few weeks, and I learned her real name was Sandy Luby. She'd grown up in Carbondale, Illinois where she shared a tiny studio apartment with her mother. Determined to marry a millionaire, she applied to become an international flight attendant the day she turned eighteen.

"It's bound to happen," she said. "I date so many of them, like John. He's already married, but that could change." She started on a second bottle of wine as we picked at our shrimp salads in the dining room at The Plaza where she'd taken me to lunch on John's credit card.

I told Alex I'd come to New York to pursue a career in musical theatre, but for the moment I'd run out of money for classes. When Jimmie and Judy were out of the apartment, I practiced my vocal exercises instead.

"With your looks, you should go after a wealthy man while you're still young. You're crazy to waste your time at low-paying shit jobs trying to make it as a performer. You don't want to end up like the rest of the pathetic forty-year-olds in this town still hoping for their big break."

"Jimmie tells me I'm not the type for musical theatre. I'm too tall. 'Think about it,' he'd said, 'Bernadette Peters, Liza Minnelli, Barbra Streisand, all short.'"

"That's ridiculous and if you really want to go for it, I'll introduce you to Sam Spiegel."

"The movie producer?"

"Yeah, you know, *On the Waterfront, Bridge on the River Kwai, Lawrence of Arabia*? If he can't help you, no one can." She said he was an old friend of hers whom she'd met on a flight from New York to Paris and she'd spent time on his yacht in the French Riviera.

Sam Spiegel was old all right, probably around seventy. I could tell Alex had slept with him. She jumped in his lap as soon as he sat down. At his request, I sang, "What'll I Do," standing by the baby grand as light from a chandelier sparkled on its shiny black surface. The butler played the song from sheet music while Alex, still sitting in his lap, stroked Sam's face. After I finished, he said, "Fantastic. You have great energy for performing."

That's what David had said and why he'd insisted I move to New York.

I wasn't sure why I slept with Sam the following week when I went to his Park Avenue apartment alone on a rainy night. I drank several martinis. Opulence oozed from the walls, which were lined with Chagalls, Picassos, and Miros. I didn't want to leave. I could have stayed for days to study the art. My favorite Chagall painting, "Lovers in the Red Sky," an image of a woman and her lover flying against a vibrant red background, hung above his bed.

The morning after, I told him I had to find a new place

to live. I didn't expect money, but he offered to put me up at the Barbizon Hotel for Women. I'd passed by the run-down hotel and once ate a dry sweet roll in the coffee shop.

"In its heyday, the Barbizon was home to artists, writers, and actresses who came to New York to pursue their careers."

What actresses had slept with him in exchange for parts in his movies?

He asked if I wanted something to eat and led me to the dining room overlooking Central Park. A hazy band of sunlight settled over the blanket of treetops. A woman in a maid's uniform brought blueberry pancakes, scrambled eggs, sausage, bacon, bagels, lox and cream cheese, waffles, and coffee to the dining table, which was covered in white linen and big silver cutlery.

After breakfast, he lit a cigar and rubbed my thigh as he puffed. He opened his monogrammed, navy blue silk robe and put my hand on his penis. I massaged it, but I didn't want to go down on him again, which I knew he wanted. I'd done that earlier only because he'd told me I was a little selfish in bed. And even then, I had to get drunk to oblige him.

"You must have been something at fifteen," he said.

I told him I had an appointment and had to leave. He pulled out $500 and a card from his pocket. "Call my business manager when you run out of money. I'll be shooting in Europe for several months. And buy yourself some rain boots." The butler walked me to the door.

Before I left Jimmie's apartment, I made tiny knife slits in his leather couch that would open wide over time.

# Mrs. Burden

The Barbizon's magnificence had faded. But the lobby, the soundproof music rooms, artists' studios, and library on the mezzanine floor still felt very grand, cloistered, and exclusive. It smelled like the plush carpeting and dark polished wood of what I imagined was glamorous, old New York. But the rooms and the upper floors had ceiling stains and the damask wallpaper was peeling.

My closet-sized, dingy, pink and green room had a tiny desk, a shallow two-drawer dresser, and an outdated radio speaker on the wall. My grandmother's vintage wool suits from the 1940s that I'd brought from Phoenix and the disco dancing beaded outfits David had made were jammed into the closet and piled high in a corner. An ancient bathroom to share with thirty other rooms, mostly empty, loomed at the end of a dimly lit hallway. There were no suites or kitchenettes. Cooking of any kind was forbidden. An overpriced coffee shop on the street level was the only convenient place to eat. I hadn't seen anyone watching, but the guy at the front desk told me that men were not allowed above the lobby when I'd moved in two weeks ago.

I spent time lying on the narrow single bed, my feet and

ankles hanging off the end, recounting my life. I refused to believe my destiny was to scratch out a living, working temp jobs while taking classes for the dream of performing on Broadway. Snow collected on the window ledge where I'd tied six small cartons of blueberry yogurt and a half pint of milk with string, pulled the ends through the sides of the window, and anchored them to the desk drawer knobs so they wouldn't blow away. I had little cash left for food after eating two week's worth of meals in the coffee shop. I snuck in a small hot plate and saucepan to heat up soup and water for instant coffee.

Sylvia Plath's feet must have hung off the end of the bed, too, when she stayed here in 1953 after winning the guest editorship contest from *Mademoiselle* magazine. I read she was five-foot-nine. I pictured her in bobbed hair, wearing a suit with a straight skirt below the knee, white gloves and a little hat, excited to be in the city, seizing her life as a writer before depression consumed her.

A year ago, I was ready to grasp everything New York had to offer, but without family support, a trust fund, or a benefactor, all I could see ahead of me was more secretarial work, waitressing, and hostessing. I had natural talent for painting, dancing, and acting. But why continue to pursue any of that? I'd never make enough money.

My friend Alex had the right idea: to marry a million-aire and deal with the bargains, no matter how shitty. She eventually married Douglas, a billionaire, Texas oilman with whom I'd gone to high school. I'd introduced them. He'd grown tired of prostitutes and was desperate for a real girlfriend. He'd had a crush on me since we conjugated verbs in Mrs. Stone's Spanish class, but there was something scary about the look in his eyes, so I avoided him. Douglas beat up Alex in Saudi Arabia on their honeymoon because she flirted with one of the princes. She probably thought she could nab the prince, who had more money than Douglas. There must have been other beatings, but Alex never talked about them. She had everything else she'd ever wanted.

No matter how many jobs I worked, I'd never survive on my own. I'd still be living at my perverted cousin's place if Sam hadn't given me money.

I watched my milk and yogurt cartons disappear under heavy falling snow and decided to conduct an experiment. *I'll do nothing*, I thought. As Kafka said, I'll stay still and alone, and wait for the world to come to me.

I heated up a can of tomato soup.

The guy at the front desk called to tell me I had another message from Diane, my agent at Career Blazers Temp Agency. He said, "Honey, she says she has jobs for you!" His voice was emphatic with exclamation points. "You need to call her!"

The next day, I told Diane to take me off her list.

"What will you do for money?"

"I don't know. I'm going to wait for a sign from God or the universe or … someone or something must know the coordinates of where I'm staying."

"A sign of what?"

"Of whatever's next. I can't keep doing what I've been doing."

"It sounds scary. But okay, if you change your mind, call me right away. I can always find work for you."

At the end of the month, I ran out of money and called Sam's business manager.

"We have an arrangement he said you'd know about," I said.

"I don't know anything. He's out of town."

"Can you call him?"

"There's nothing I can do for you," he said and hung up.

I should have known Sam wouldn't keep his word. If he could get teenage girls to have sex with him, why would he bother with me? I didn't want his damn money anyway.

I told the Barbizon I was waiting for a check and asked if I could pay my rent in a week's time. They agreed. Two weeks went by. Waves of dizziness and nausea slammed through my body when past due notices began to appear under my door.

One day, Diane called again. "I have an emergency. No one else will fit the bill. I know you said not to call, but you have to go."

"Go where?"

"It's a secretarial job with a law enforcement philanthropist. It's only for two weeks while his secretary goes on vacation."

"No, I'm not temping anymore."

"Please. You're the only one who has any class. I'm begging you, as a favor to me. Then I won't call again. I promise."

"Oh, all right, I'll do it, but what the hell is a law enforcement philanthropist?"

"I have no idea, but his secretary told me he's a descendent of the Vanderbilt family."

\*\*\*

At the top floor of Ordway Burden's building on the Upper East Side, his secretary, Sally, wearing an A-line skirt and penny loafers, greeted me at the door of his apartment. The furnishings were nondescript, like a hotel.

Sally led me to one of two bedrooms that shared a wall. The master had been converted into an office.

"You work so close to where he sleeps?" I asked.

"Oh, you don't have to worry about anything like that. He won't bother you. This isn't a real job," she said. "It's mostly ordering things he circles in catalogs and mailing out checks to law enforcement agencies."

"Why does he do that?"

"He receives plaques and badges in return. You might spend a whole day arranging them on the walls of the apartment next door. It's his personal museum."

"Wow."

"Besides your salary, you get 200 a week in petty cash in case he wants a sandwich or needs more liquor or whatever."

Sally peered at me over the top of her red-rimmed glasses and cleared her throat. "Usually, there's money left over at the end of the week. Sometimes, I treat myself to a steak on Friday night."

We went next door to the "museum," another two-bedroom apartment, empty except for low wooden benches in the center of each room. The stark white walls were loaded top to bottom with black-framed certificates and oak wood plaques, engraved gold plates on their fronts.

Ordway appeared from around the corner: tall, about thirty, wearing an ill-fitting toupee, holding a drink in one hand and a stack of small leather cases in the other. "Badges," he said and laid them out on one of the benches.

Sally had told me he was so wealthy he didn't have to do anything, let alone make money, and that he drank gin and tonics all day. From the look of his red wandering eyes, he'd had several.

I stretched my arm out, extending my whole shoulder as far from myself as possible, and shook his clammy, shaky hand.

"Showing her the ropes?" he said to Sally. He sipped his drink and looked at me wryly. "Think you can get along with all these cops and sheriffs?" He waved his soft white hand in a circle around the room and half smiled. He seemed to want praise, and at the same time, his smile let me know he was prepared to make a joke, depending on my reaction.

"I think so," I said.

"How do you like the museum?"

"Very unique. I've never seen anything like it."

"Thank you." He faced the window and rocked back and forth on his stiff feet.

Sally said he'd interviewed two women from another agency. If he chose me, I'd take the job. Two hundred fifty a week was much more than I could earn at a regular temp job. I could stay at the Barbizon a while longer.

"It was nice to meet both of you," I said at the door.

Ordway turned slightly and raised his glass to me as if he'd made up his mind.

\*\*\*

Every morning there was a "to-do" list on the brand new IBM Selectric typewriter: "Call the sheriff in Greensboro, North Carolina; find out where my badges are; call my mother and find out what time I'm expected for dinner; unpack the plaques that came in the mail and see me about where to hang them."

Ordway sat at his desk, read law enforcement magazines, and circled items in catalogs for me to order. I picked up his cleaning and made trips to the liquor store for Beefeater gin and inexpensive Bolla Valpolicella wine. He told me he liked seeing the word police on the label.

Sally didn't come back from her Trinidad vacation. She fell in love with a steel pan musician and decided to stay there. Ordway asked me if I wanted a full-time job. Not what I expected to writhe at my feet, but I accepted his offer as the sign I'd been waiting for.

I paid my back rent at the Barbizon and with the extra petty cash, ate out. I worked from noon, when Ordway got up, to six. I had time to take dance classes again and practice vocal exercises in one of the Barbizon's music rooms.

Soon, I'd be able to rent my own apartment.

\*\*\*

One day, Ordway asked me to go to Hammacher Schlemmer to buy a birthday gift for his mother. He showed me the catalog in which he'd circled a picture of an electric vacuum record cleaner. "My parents have a collection of old Tom Lehrer records," he said. "This is perfect."

"Didn't he sing a song about dope peddlers?" I remembered a boy in high school playing Tom Lehrer records at parties.

"That's him."

"And your parents like his songs?"

"They do." He moved his chair closer to my desk. "Here," he said, pointing to a picture of a Lucite paperweight in the shape of an X. "This would be good for my father's birthday in a couple months. You'd better get this too. They might run out."

I asked if he had any siblings who might need a gift.

He told me his eldest brother had shot himself over his unfaithful wife some years ago.

"Oh, I'm so sorry."

"My other older brother is a schizophrenic and lives with two caregivers. My younger brother became a teacher at a private boys school after he left the army. He's a closeted homosexual. My father had very different expectations for his sons."

Ordway told me his parents owned a summer home in Northeast Harbor, Maine and an estate in Mt. Kisco, complete with a bomb shelter.

\*\*\*

On a gray, cloudy Monday, Ordway's mother, Peggy, whom I hadn't met, called me at the Barbizon and asked if I could go to work early. She'd talked to Ordway and he sounded depressed. "He's had some bad episodes, dearie. I would go, but he won't let me in. You're the only one with a set of keys."

I took a cab, let myself in, and knocked on his bedroom door. Having to handle this situation was not part of my job description. Peggy hadn't mentioned suicide, but what if he'd overdosed on something? He took at least eight prescription pills a day. Did he have guns? What if he'd shot himself like his brother? I was afraid I might find his brains on the floor.

I'd felt suicidal before. It never lasted for more than a week. Nobody paid attention, especially not my mother, other than the one time she sent her Christian Scientist boyfriend to my apartment to read to me from Mary Baker Eddy's *Science and Health* as if that would cure my unhappiness.

I heard noise in his bedroom. I waited in the office as

sheets of rain pelted against the window. My eyes focused back and forth between the wet sealed off city and my solitary reflection dissected by running water streaming down the glass.

Ordway emerged dressed in his usual white Brooks Brothers shirt, red tie, suspenders, dark pin-stripe suit, and wingtip shoes. He ducked into the bathroom. When he came out, his toupee was crooked and his face puffy. He sat at his desk and silently opened his mail. I wanted to leave but decided to stay and act normally. I read the note he'd left me to type a letter to the sheriff in Cleveland, Tennessee to ask about a speaking engagement. There was also a pile of newspaper and periodical clippings that recounted the difficulties of inherited wealth and the ills of the dysfunctional children of the rich, torn out or circled with instructions to Xerox them and send to everyone in his Rolodex.

The next day at work, there were flowers on my desk with a note of apology.

"Are you okay?" I asked.

"Fine."

"Your mother said you were depressed."

"I wish she'd mind her own business. It's not your problem."

It was my problem. I seemed to be the only person he saw on a regular basis. From now on, I'd be in a state of unwanted hyper-vigilance about his emotional state.

He ripped open an envelope. "My mother shouldn't have called you. It happens sometimes."

If helping him process his episodes of depression was going to be part of my job, I would have to ask for a raise. "I know what you mean."

He swiveled his chair around and faced me. "You do?"

"Life doesn't ever seem to turn out the way it should."

"What do you do about it?"

"Different things. Sometimes I eat."

Ordway laughed. Sheets of his official embossed stationery floated to the floor as his hand accidentally grazed the desk.

"I hold my breath and hope the feeling goes away quickly," he said.

"How often does it happen?"

"Occasionally."

"Well, how about some food? I could make you something."

"Oh, no. I never eat at home. Let's go out, or I could order in."

"You have a few things in the refrigerator. I could make open-faced cheese and tomato sandwiches."

He laughed. "What's that?"

"Something my mother used to make. Only one slice of bread so you don't get fat."

"I guess I could use some help with that," he said, patting his stomach. "But I'd like to take you out. What's your pleasure?"

"I don't know about that," I said.

"We'll make it a business lunch. I'd like your opinion on an idea I have for a speech I have to give for my Dale Carnegie class. I'm working on my public speaking skills."

"Well, okay."

"I'll change into something more casual."

He returned a few minutes later in a sheriff's outfit: khaki pants, brown shirt, badge, black boots, and a Stetson hat. A set of holsters on his hips held two ivory-handled guns.

I knocked over my coffee cup. Not knowing whether to laugh or scream, I covered my mouth. I didn't want to set him off. He could have another episode; shoot me and himself this time.

He stood in the doorway and shifted his weight from foot to foot, turning his head as if wanting me to see his profile in the hat. He licked his lips and waited for a response.

"That's quite an outfit," I said, searching his face for a sign that this was a joke.

"I haven't worn it out before. I wanted you to see it." He smiled and put his hands over the guns.

"Are those loaded?"

"Sure," he said.

"Is it legal to go to a restaurant in New York with two loaded guns on your hips? I mean, it's a great look, but I'd feel better if you took them off."

"Oh." His shoulders dropped. "I called a limo. It should be downstairs any minute."

"A limo? Where are we going? Maybe it'd be better if we stayed here and ordered in."

"No." He took a wider stance, one heavy boot at a time. "I made reservations and …" The doorman rang the buzzer. "The limo is here. It's too late to cancel." He undid the holster and carefully laid it out on the couch. I assumed he wouldn't eat with the hat on. Without that and the guns, his weird costume was somewhat dismantled.

In the limo, I slid my thighs across buttery black leather and heard Alex's voice, *Here's your chance.*

Ordway mixed a gin and tonic, stirred it slowly with a red swivel stick, and handed it to me. He made one for himself and leaned his head back on a rolled leather pillow. The driver turned into Central Park. "See," Ordway said, pointing out the black-tinted window at a cop on a horse. "Central Park Police. They have one of the best precincts."

"Does each guy take care of his own horse?"

"Sure. The horse is a partner."

I didn't understand his interest in cops and sheriffs, but he teared up when he talked about their sacrifices and courage. He'd recently set up a non-profit called the National Law Enforcement Assistance Fund to help the families of officers who died or were injured in the line of duty. Did he crave the discipline and structure of law enforcement? He had no rules he had to follow, didn't have to live up to anyone's standards. But he obviously liked uniforms.

At Luigi's, he ordered a bottle of wine. "What's your pleasure?" he asked, scanning the menu.

"I like spaghetti with garlic and oil."

"Excellent choice."

I could tell by the way people in the restaurant stared at us, they thought Ordway looked strange and that I was his date. His height and nice features helped, but the bad toupee and the outfit ruined everything. After three glasses of wine, I decided to be honest with him.

"You know, I think you'd look better without the toupee."

"I'm so used to it," he said.

"Do you ever wear turtlenecks?"

"Well, no."

"Navy blue would be a nice color."

"I'll consider that. Maybe you'd come with me some-time to one of the conventions. They're quite something."

"I'll bet they are."

"I'm sure you'd have fun."

Alex would have advised me to seduce him in the

restaurant, go back to his apartment and have sex. But the most important thing for me was to get my own apartment. I didn't have to sleep with him for that. I'd found a place on 72nd and Columbus, on the corner above a chicken take-out place and Pier 1 Imports, near the Dakota, where John Lennon owned an apartment. I didn't yet have enough money for the deposit and first and last month's rent.

I'd been thinking about asking Ordway to loan it to me. After coming to work early, dealing with his episode, and eating lunch with him, I thought now would be the perfect time.

"How much do you need?"

"Nine hundred to move in. I'll pay you back as soon as I can."

"Don't worry about it." He pulled out a money clip, counted out nine hundred-dollar bills, and handed them to me. The couple at the next table cleared their throats. Crooked half smiles appeared on their faces as they made snickering noises at each other.

Ordway pulled out a stack of index cards with the tiniest little black marks I'd ever seen from the inside pocket of his sheriff's jacket. "Do you want to hear the idea for my speech now? I'm nervous about it. I'm afraid my heart will stop."

"I'm ready."

"The title is *Community to City: A Perspective of American Law Enforcement.* So far, I have three points."

"Okay. The title is good."

"Point one: The American sheriff summoned posses to pursue criminals or squelch insurrections and supervised the empanelment of juries. Point two: Familiarity in villages worked against the commission of crime, by making community approval desirable."

His hands shook as he shuffled through the index cards.

"Point three: The idea of a policeman as primarily a crime fighter did not evolve until well into this century, given much impetus by the Prohibition-era gangster."

"What do you think?"

"Interesting," I said. "I've never thought about the history of law enforcement."

"It's fascinating," he said.

"I'm sure your audience will agree."

\*\*\*

I hadn't talked to David since he and his lover, John, moved in together. They invited me out once, but I didn't like John. He was a boring, bucktoothed hick from the Midwest.

When he called David "sweetheart," I tried to swallow the bitter tang in my mouth.

When I moved out of the Barbizon, I asked David to help me decorate my new place. I had hoped we could be together without John.

My one-bedroom apartment had gleaming wood floors and freshly painted white walls. I lined the big window that faced the building next door with ivy and wandering jew plants. David and I spent four days hanging the authentic 1930s calla lily wallpaper he'd discovered in an antique store while, with a tinge of regret, we sang "Ain't No Mountain High Enough," and "Break Up to Make Up," two of the songs we'd planned to sing in our act, our harmonizing still intact. He also found a 1940s blond wood dressing table with blue glass drawer pulls, once used for stage sets at the Met, a matching dresser, and two rattan deck chairs rescued from a cruise ship. I put a deposit down on the furniture and started hoarding petty cash.

At first, I wrote down the amounts I saved in a ledger, thinking I'd pay it back. Ordway wouldn't mind. I had to deal with his strange behavior and I wasn't getting paid extra for that. I told him I needed more petty cash.

"Oh, how much more?" he said.

"Fifty dollars?"

"How about a hundred? Why don't we make it 300 a week from now on? I'll put you on the signature card at the bank. It's easier that way, and if you need more during the week you'll be authorized to withdraw it."

"Okay," I said.

Each month I paid off one piece of furniture. I bought a queen-sized bed to replace the foam pad I'd been sleeping on. There was no end to the things I needed: a coat, boots and shoes, dishes, dining table, cookware, rugs, and curtains.

Salespeople would ask, "Will this be on your charge?"

"Cash," I'd say and flip open my wallet, the bills facing the same way, like Ordway kept his. I'd leave the stores feeling exhilarated, very rich, and like a member of the Burden family. I'd been able to talk myself out of the fact that I was stealing by telling myself I deserved the money and Ordway had so much it didn't matter. But as guilt began to bleed through my justifications, he seemed less bizarre and I began to imagine having a relationship with him.

After I bought a glass coffee table, I told myself I'd start paying back the money. But David insisted I buy the gold trimmed, pink depression glassware he'd found in the Village.

He told me he still loved me and wanted to be in my life.

"That would be too difficult for me," I said.

"But there are so many women who fall in love with gay men," he said. "It's no big deal." He laughed. Had my love for him become a joke? I decided not to see him again. I had to move on.

After work, I'd usually pick up dinner at the chicken place below my building: a breast, a thigh, coleslaw, and a bagel. On weekends, I read the *New York Times* entertainment section and made a list of all the things I wanted to do. But now that David was gone, I didn't have anyone to go with.

\*\*\*

At Moi's, a skin and nail salon on the Upper East Side, I met a trim woman with short, blonde hair and delicate features. She wore an expensive business suit.

"I like that color," she said watching the manicurist turn my toenails burgundy red. "Do you think I should try it?"

"I do. We have the same coloring."

"Do you come here often?" she asked.

"It depends on how much money I have at the end of the week. This is my second time."

"I come every week for something. I'm in advertising. I charge the services to my expense account. Know what I mean?"

"Oh, yes." Maybe I could talk to this woman about my situation with Ordway.

"Do you work?"

"As a personal secretary."

"I think I will try that color. It makes me want to drink a glass of Merlot."

"Why don't we get one after this," I said.

"Terrific. My name is Vicki."

"I'm Linda."

"By the way, have you tried waxing? It's fabulous."

\*\*\*

In June, Ordway's gay brother, Bob, died in a car crash. A semi-truck smashed into his car. Ordway didn't believe it was an accident. "He was recently accused of molesting one of his students. I think he wanted to end it."

Ordway expressed no emotion in front of me but asked if I'd go with him to his parents' place so he could pay his respects. It seemed an odd way to meet them for the first time, but I felt obligated.

The butler greeted us at the door of the Fifth Avenue penthouse. Ordway whispered, "My father likes him because he worked at the White House and Buckingham Palace." Water dripped from the gold fountain in the entryway. I thought I heard muffled crying. Rauschenberg, Pollack, Warhol, and Rothko hung on the walls. Ordway's father had been president of the Museum of Modern Art in the '50s and '60s. He was elected after his friend, Nelson Rockefeller, resigned.

Ordway led me to the dining room where his parents, Peggy and Bill, and his brother, Hamilton, sat. Two women in maid's uniforms served food. Black candles and wine glasses lined the middle of the table. Ordway's mother said, "Nice to meet you, dearie. Please join us."

"I'm so sorry for your loss," I said.

Ordway's brainy, quirky father and brother didn't say a word. All the Burden men had unusually high foreheads.

"We just stopped by for a minute," said Ordway. He shuffled me out as quickly as possible.

For my birthday, Ordway gave me a Steuben glass giraffe—I'd told him I loved giraffes—and took me to lunch at the Russian Tea Room for caviar. In August, he invited me to cool off for a weekend in Northeast Harbor. He would be there for the month. The heat in the city was unbearable. My portable fan moved hot, sticky air through the apartment until it broke.

He met me at the Bar Harbor Airport in his antique Aston Martin convertible. His toupee flipped off the front of his head and stuck straight up in the wind. Other than that, he looked almost daring in his dark-mirrored sunglasses, set off by the upturned collar of his navy blue blazer with the gold and red crest on the pocket. Underneath it, he wore one of the turtlenecks I'd picked out for him.

"I've never been to Maine."

"I know all the policemen in Bar Harbor."

"Oh."

"That's a nice dress."

"Thank you. It's new." I was glad he liked it since he'd paid for it. I had a choking sensation and put my hand over my throat. Trapped in guilt, thinking of all the money I'd taken, I concentrated on a piece of sky, pine trees, and the water hitting against black rocks on the shoreline.

"Are you all right?'

"Oh, I'm fine." I cleared my throat and took a deep breath.

The summer breeze soothed my hot city skin. The sky darkened. Black rocks turned into menacing shapes.

"My mother's looking forward to seeing you again. My friend, Ralph, from college, is here for the weekend too."

He pulled off the highway onto a dirt road. Nestled in

the pine trees was a large house and several cottages over-looking the water, all painted a light coastal gray.

"Well, here we are."

The ceiling of the living room in the main house was sculpted in waves of sloping wood and had the illusion of meeting the ocean waves outside. Peggy and Bill each sat under a pink spotlight, a round disk that fanned light out from the ceiling over their chairs. The old poodle had one, too, shining on his favorite spot on the carpet. Ordway and his brothers evidently didn't have a spotlight.

"Get the binoculars. Show her Nelson's house," said Bill.

They were all in various stages of drunkenness.

"My father has always wanted to be a Rockefeller," Ordway whispered to me. He went to the bar to make drinks. I asked for a strong Scotch and water.

"So, you're the secretary," said Ralph. He looked me up and down and put his arm around my shoulders.

I turned sideways, slipped out from under his hug and knelt down to pet the dog.

By the time dinner was announced, Peggy and Bill needed help getting to the boomerang shaped dining table that matched the curved lines of the ceiling. I sat between Ordway and his father, across from Ralph.

Peggy picked at her food. "Just two bites of each thing. It's the secret to staying thin. Isn't that right, dearie?"

"That's what my mother says."

Her bleary eyes wandered in my direction. "You're such a pretty girl."

"Thank you."

"And so cosmopolitan. I approve, Ordway."

"Meet us at the boat tomorrow, nine o'clock sharp," said Bill. He balanced a piece of duck on his fork and aimed it at his mouth. It fell in mid-air and plopped back on his plate.

"I have a meeting in town tomorrow," said Ordway.

"I don't know what you see in those people," Bill said.

Ordway's face reddened, his jaw tightened.

"He's helping them," I said.

Ordway smiled at me.

"He doesn't need to be there. Captain will meet you at the dock," said Bill.

"Is Captain his first name?" I asked.

"It is to us. He'll fix eggs and sausage for breakfast in the galley and whip up the best clam chowder you've ever tasted for our picnic lunch."

Ralph tried to touch my leg with his toes. He'd removed his shoe, and all I could feel was the edge of something sharp, probably an untrimmed nail. I scooted my chair back, away from Ralph's foot.

After dinner, the Spanish cook served coffee in the living room.

"Thank you for a wonderful dinner, Peggy," I said. "Please excuse me. I'm very tired."

"Of course, dearie. We'll see you tomorrow."

I walked into the green black night down the dirt road to my designated cottage, ignoring unfamiliar dark shapes that loomed up on either side of the path. I heard footsteps behind me, thinking Ralph had followed me. I turned. It was Ordway, the outline of his blue blazer more defined as he came closer.

"May I walk you to your cottage?"

He offered me his arm, and I took it.

The beds in the cottage had been turned down, a rose and two small gold-wrapped chocolates placed on the pillows.

I hadn't expected rip-roaring love making from him but I imagined more than I got. I chalked up his lackadaisical performance of half-heartedly sucking on my right breast and quick ejaculation to having drunk too many gin and tonics. I'd had plenty to drink too. Before he passed out, he told me it'd been a long time since he'd been with a woman who wasn't a prostitute. His therapist had been encouraging him to start dating.

"I'll never forget this," he said.

I drifted off, wondering which category I fit into. For the first time in months, I slept guilt free.

When I woke the next morning, Ordway was gone. I dressed and walked the long path to the boat dock. Captain, dressed in a khaki uniform, shook my hand and said, "So you're Ordway's new girlfriend. He didn't come with you? Poor guy, he's afraid of the boat and the water, even as a little boy."

"I'm his secretary," I said.

"Well, you could be the girlfriend. If I squint my eyes, you kind of resemble Brooke Shields. You have short hair but you're the same height. You must know he has the most extensive collection of Brooke Shields memorabilia in the world."

"No, I didn't."

"You're older, though. I can tell by your legs. I can always tell the age of a woman by the look of her legs."

"Is that so?" I was sorry I'd worn shorts. I ignored his gaze by looking at the sea, focusing on the glistening diamond-like light.

Before long, Ralph and the Burdens, each holding either arm of their caregiver, arrived on the dock, interrupting Captain's harassment.

Captain's addictive "signature" daiquiris began to flow. I lost count of how many the Burdens drank. I had six, which made it easier to pretend I belonged around these wealthy, crazy people. Bill talked tearfully about his lifelong dream of being ambassador to France until he nodded off in a deck chair.

At Placentia Island, Captain landed *Spindrift,* and we went ashore for a picnic of clam chowder and more booze. How did these people drink so much? I went behind a small sand dune and made myself throw up, something my grandmother taught me to do when I was a teenager. I felt better but still woozy on the boat ride back.

***

In my cottage, I packed my things. I put on my grandmother's 1940s hand-painted, sequined dress splashed with images of the Hawaiian Islands that she'd worn for dinner on the cruise ships she and my grandfather used to take to Oahu. I walked to the big house for the family's famous lobster dinner, caught by Captain in the Burden's own trap. The buttery crustacean melted in my mouth. Ordway gave me quirky winks—meant to be affectionate—at the dining table. Geeky and lonely, he must have been longing for connection with a woman. I wasn't sure I could oblige, but I'd have all the money I would ever need or want. I debated if putting up with what I'd experienced in the past two days was worth it.

After dinner, Ordway drove me to the airport for my flight back to New York. "Sorry you have to go, but there are calls to make and letters to type at the office. We can't get too behind on things." Ordway kissed me goodbye. "I'll miss you, but I'll return on Labor Day," he said.

I was anxious to get on the plane, to be alone and think things through.

***

I searched his apartment for the Brooke Shields memorabilia. I couldn't find any, but a stockpile of pornographic magazines was hidden under his mattress. Most of it was soft porn and not too offensive.

I got in the habit of only taking cabs. I met Vicki at the spa for a massage and facial. Afterwards, we went out for drinks. I told her I'd had sex with my boss but not about taking his money.

"How was it?" she asked.

"Not great, but that house in Maine is to die for."

"Well, we can't have everything, right?"

"I guess not."

Vicki gulped down the last of her wine and ordered another glass. "On second thought, I might be wrong. I just signed up for the est training."

I ordered a second Scotch and water. "The what?"

"It's an intensive consciousness seminar. Supposedly, in two weekends, everyone has a transformational experience."

What could she possibly want to change about her life? She had a great paying job as a copywriter—something she loved—at one of the top advertising agencies; an expense account; she traveled worldwide to places where her agency shot the commercials she wrote. She rented a house on Fire Island every summer. Her office had a view of the city. Large palm plants lived next to her Lucite desk. Her parents were loving and supportive; she'd had a private school education. Her father was horrified when he asked and I told him I didn't have health or apartment insurance. Vicki said he and her mother adored me. I thought they felt sorry for me.

"Transformation of what?" I asked.

"I'll let you know."

\*\*\*

Ordway called every day for updates and with a new list of tasks. He said he was dying to kiss me, make love to me again, and take me to dinner, a Broadway show or wherever I wanted to go. My affection for him grew.

He came back to town the day before Labor Day. His parents had returned a few days earlier and checked into New York Hospital for a week of drying out, something they did every year in early September, planned around their chef's vacation. They had all their meals catered by their favorite restaurants: La Caravelle, the Four Seasons, Le Cygne, The Palm, and La Grenouille. Over the next few months, Ordway took me to all of them. They were his favorites too.

During the workday, he'd ask me to sit on his lap and kiss him. Sometimes that led to sex, which had become more passionate, and I'd stay overnight.

Every time we had sex, he said, "I'll never forget this."

My desire for performing had diminished over the past year, but I told myself I was still in the game. Ordway took me to the Broadway shows I couldn't afford to see on my own. I loved the songs, especially, "Magic to Do," Bob Fosse's choreography, and the upbeat story of *Pippin,* but related more to the complex psychological dramas of *Equus* and *The Elephant Man.*

In October, Ordway invited me to go with him to the sheriff conventions in Portland and Las Vegas. "We could stop in Scottsdale if you want to see your family," he said.

Who would I visit? My grandmother? She rarely left her house or let anyone in. My sister? We hadn't been close since we were kids. Whenever I spoke with my mother, she gave me an update on Kimberly about whatever man was currently in her life. The last one I'd heard about was Ken, who my mother said was "basically very bright," just needed a "little cleaning up." She said she loaned him money and along with the $10,000 Kimberly gave him from her divorce, he started a collection agency business. Kimberly found out he'd been dealing drugs when he went out at night, not collecting property people hadn't paid for. I had no hope that her life would take a better turn.

It'd been months since I'd talked to my mother. Each time I called to tell her about my New York adventures—the few auditions I landed; encouraging feedback from dance teachers and my vocal coach; the singing/dancing act with David; leaving David; temp jobs; staying with cousin Jimmie; the Barbizon—no matter what I shared, she'd groan with disapproval and say, "Do you really think that's a good idea?" I'd hang up, questioning my choices. *Why was I here?* Enveloped in a dark, heavy cloud for days afterwards, I'd fight off suicidal thoughts.

By the time I started working for Ordway, I'd stopped calling her; and she wasn't in the habit of calling me. She knew nothing about him or my new apartment.

I decided to call and tell her, knowing she'd be jealous but wouldn't criticize. The idea of him and his wealthy family was everything she'd ever wanted for herself.

"Oh my god, a Vanderbilt? Have you told your grandmother? This is so exciting. When can I meet him? I think I'm going to tinkle in my pants."

I imagined the three of us drunk, definitely a requirement, sitting in her condo after eating her bad cooking; she, awkward, husbandless once again, chain smoking, chatting non-stop, bragging about her close friendships with the tennis stars that lived in the building, how well known she was around town, and how wealthy her father had been. A sad picture I had no desire to make a reality.

At the sheriff convention in Portland, I had fun dancing to country music with Sheriff Buck Slayton who chanted his slogan, "Vote for Buck, he's our friend," as he spun me around the dance floor.

In Vegas, Red Mobley told me it was unknown for a time whether his opponent would be Ted Rumford or Fred Farley. "Lucky for me both names rhyme with Red," he said. During the weekend of the convention, a group of his singing supporters sang from the back of a pickup truck as it rolled slowly down the streets of old Las Vegas, "It's Red we want, not Fred."

\*\*\*

For Christmas, Ordway gave me a full-length stone marten mink coat, my initials embroidered into the lining. My shock catapulted me into believing that I, and not my mother, had always wanted one. At fourteen, I did imagine myself wearing the Russian sable coat I saw in the December issue of my mother's *Vogue* magazine, silvery gray streaked through brown fur, fluffier, softer than a stone marten. Though paltry in comparison, Ordway loved my gift of a pair of cute hand-painted ceramic baby pigs dressed in cop uniforms.

I invited Vicki to lunch at 21 Club so I could show her my mink.

"We'll never get a reservation this time of year," she said.

"I can get one."

Ordway had taken me there two weeks earlier. Among the cast-iron jockey statues that adorn the balcony above the entrance, each representing a wealthy family's horse farm, Ordway pointed out the one painted in "diamond white" and "cerise," the colors of the Vanderbilt stables racing silks.

The maître d' referred to me as Mrs. Burden. Ordway didn't correct him, and neither did I.

Now, without a second thought, I called 21 Club and reserved a table for Mrs. Burden. Wearing the mink and my favorite gold and pearl ring on my left hand, turned backwards to show just the band, given to me by my ex-step-father, Jack, I met Vicki for lunch as a married woman. Impressed with my subterfuge and my coat, she said, "We'll have to do this more often. I wonder what kind of winter wrap I could justify putting on my expense account."

\*\*\*

After finishing a bottle of Champagne at his apartment, Ordway and I took a cab to the Four Seasons for a late New Year's Eve dinner. We drank more Champagne and ate Oregon Caviar with Blinis. Caviar was my new favorite food.

By the time we left the restaurant, it was pouring rain. All the cabs were taken, and he'd forgotten to book a limo. "This is devastating," he said.

"We can take the bus."

"I can't do that."

"Why not?"

"I don't know which bus to take." He started pacing around a puddle.

"I do. It stops right on the corner of your street."

"No, I can't. I have no change."

"I have tokens."

"Tokens?"

"For the subway. They're good on buses too." I dug to

the bottom of my purse and pulled them out. "See," I said, laying them out in my palm.

"I can't," he said.

"There's the bus now. Let's go." I grabbed his arm, pulled at him to follow me. His umbrella flipped inside out in the wet wind.

I nudged him up the bus's steep steps. The driver lurched into traffic. Ordway almost fell before squeezing himself into a seat next to an old man. I stood in front of him, dripping wet. He clutched the arm of the seat, twisted his head back and forth, and pulled his legs tighter and tighter together. His eyes darted everywhere.

I touched his arm, and he jumped.

"Are you okay?"

"Don't touch me. I'm trying to stay alive right now."

"Here we are," I said. I was trembling from the cold and fear of what he might do. "It's only a short walk to your place from here."

He bolted from the bus and zoomed out ahead of me. I ran behind him, my raincoat blowing, twisting around my body. I shouted through the wind and pelting rain, "What's wrong?"

By the time I got to the apartment, Ordway had secluded himself in his bedroom with the door locked. I didn't know what to do. My hands fumbled with the phone as I dialed his mother's number.

"He's in his room with the door locked." My voice caught in my throat. I wanted to run.

"What happened, dearie?"

"I don't know. He got upset on the bus."

"Bus? Oh, heavens. He's never been on a bus. Let me talk to him."

I knocked on his door and told him to pick up the phone. I heard their voices and hung up the extension.

I slept on the couch in the living room. During the night, I realized why he wanted to die. Riding a bus was so beneath him, the experience had shattered his identity. I could relate. That's how I'd felt living at the Barbizon, working as a bartender in Arizona and lowpaying shit jobs. But unlike Ordway, I didn't have the money to spend time wallowing. I either had to kill myself or keep trying to survive. For all I'd had to endure with him, I decided I'd paid back a large sum of the money I'd "borrowed."

He didn't call me over the next week, and when I went back to work after the holiday, he tried to kiss me, pretending nothing had happened.

"You scared me with that trying to stay alive business."

"It was nothing. I must have been drunk. How about dinner tonight?"

"I don't think so."

Over the next week, I declined other invitations to lunch and dinner. He got the message. I wanted out.

\*\*\*

"You can't quit," said Vicki. "You have to break it off personally. He's too crazy. But not the job. What will you do? Go back to office temp jobs or working at Brew Burger? What about your rent, facials, manicures, and cabs?"

"Yeah."

"Hang in there. Maybe I can get you a job in advertising."

Ordway stopped talking to me except about business, with an unbearable icy grumble in his voice.

Blondes with big fake boobs and toothy smiles began

to appear in photos he left on his desk, sitting on his lap at police balls and barbecues. I couldn't help but look. I'd stopped taking money, but when I saw these women, I started again.

A month later, Ordway's attorney, Harvey Silver, called and asked me if knew why there'd been an increase in Ordway's spending.

Was it my thievery? "I have no idea," I said.

"It must be the prostitutes," said Harvey. "I thought he'd stopped. See what you can do to get him to cut down."

"You must be kidding."

"I know it's awkward, but please try?"

\*\*\*

"I have to get out of there," I said to Vicki, as the smell of polish remover wafted through the salon.

"I have the perfect thing for you."

"A job?"

"Better. Remember I told you about the est training? I finished it last weekend. I realized a lot of things I was doing weren't serving me."

"Serving you?"

"It's about creating your own reality. You're the cause of the situation with Ordway. It's probably a pattern in your life."

Maybe Vicki and est were onto something, but I was torn. Part of me wanted to stay. He'd given me a peek inside the trust fund life I might have had, and I appreciated his genuine desire to help law enforcement families. If we'd both been less flawed, we might have made a go of it. But the time had come for Mrs. Burden to retire.

*Werner*

The est graduates seemed suspiciously happy, publicly displaying a level of enthusiasm I'd not seen in New York. At the same time, they were robotic in their movements, and there were so many of them, swarming like ants, out on the street, scattered over the lobby, smiling, greeting, and giving directions. I got off the elevator on the second floor. A row of them, all wearing nametags, sat at long banquet tables covered with green and beige tablecloths with perfectly boxed corners. One of them wrote my name on a nametag, another directed me to Mohegan, the ballroom for guests. Vicki, who'd convinced me to come, was shown to the Algonquin, the room for graduates.

The team in Mohegan held their arms stiffly at their sides. "Hi, Linda," they said, their eyes and smiles fixed at my nametagged left breast. "Welcome."

The chairs were perfectly lined up in even rows. The seminar leader, an ordinary looking woman in her mid-twenties with brownish-red hair and freckles, talked non-stop for thirty minutes about how her life had been transformed by the est training: her relationships with her parents, boyfriend, her job, all now worked perfectly. "It hasn't always been that way," she said. She wore an ochre colored nametag encased in plastic, her name written in calligraphy. It said, *Staff* under her name, *Connie*.

When asked about how the training worked, Connie said, "You have to actually experience it. In fact, people who don't speak English 'get it.' It's difficult to talk about. The results, however, are transformational." I wasn't sure what she meant by "experiencing." I agreed that some things were hard to talk about, but if she had no words to describe the training, what were we doing here?

Connie continued, "The actual events that occur in the training, that produce transformation, are kept secret. We ask the graduates not to divulge details. It would ruin the experience."

The only thing Vicki had told me was that you couldn't wear a watch or go to the bathroom very often, and they did something called "processes."

Connie told us a man named Werner Erhard became enlightened in March of 1971 while driving across the Golden Gate Bridge in his black Ford Mustang and started the training in his living room. "He just got it," she said.

"Got what?" asked one man.

"You have to experience it," she said. "Let's do a process."

After closing our eyes and relaxing our body parts one at time, Connie said, "Think of a time when you were sad." She paused.

I felt sad most of the time.

"Think of a time when you were happy."

That was years ago when my mother married Jack Lange, and I knew we'd finally have a happy family. Could I feel that happy again?

"Think of a time when your life worked exactly the way you wanted it to."

I couldn't think of a single thing.

"Think of a time when someone really got what you were saying, really heard your communication and understood you completely."

Nothing.

After twenty minutes, Connie had us open our eyes and said, "Would anyone be willing to share what came up for them in that process?"

After we sat for a time in silence, a woman raised her hand. She recalled a happy time at age eight, making chocolate chip cookies with her sister in an Easy-Bake Oven.

Connie asked, "What if you could feel that happy all the time?"

"I'd love it."

"That's what the training is about."

I'd love it too. Could est be the answer for relieving my pain and sadness? I never considered my life could work the way I wanted it to. I exhaled deeply.

At the end of the guest seminar, Mary, a large woman with overly permed gray hair, turned to me from the front row and stared fixedly into my eyes. "So Linda, would you like to sign up for the training?"

"I'm not sure," I said.

"Linda, did you hear anything tonight that you could relate to, that made sense to you?" Her eyes didn't blink.

"Oh, sure. I'll probably do it sometime."

I wasn't completely sold. It seemed like a repeat of what I'd read in *Psycho Cybernetics* as a teenager, about how the subconscious is out to sabotage us, to keep us from greatness. Would the results be different from the unsuccessful Nam-myoho-renge-kyo chanting David and I did for money and acting jobs, or my brief stint with Christianity and later with the Church of Religious Science? I couldn't tolerate the sad people with bad postures believing if they said affirmations all day, peace, riches, forgiveness, and satisfaction would be theirs.

*I accept financial prosperity easily and effortlessly. Spirit now clears the way for complete forgiveness. I do not judge the past. I move forward with ease and freedom.*

*Are you kidding? You're not forgiving anyone for anything,* the voice in my head answered back to these and other equally false statements.

"I have an enrollment card right here," Mary said. "You should sign up now. The trainings fill up pretty fast."

"I'm not in a hurry."

"Linda, you know how sometimes in life we decide to do something we really want to do and then if we don't do it right away we put it off and put it off and then we never do it? Does that sound familiar, Linda?"

I thought of the times I'd tried to stop stealing from Ordway.

She leaned closer to my face and lowered her voice. Her eyes were owl like. "If you sign up tonight, Linda, the results of the training will begin working in your life right away. You'll have made a real commitment to having your life work, Linda."

I signed up but questioned est's promises of a better life. At twenty-seven, maybe it wasn't too late to change. At least I wasn't joining the Moonies.

After a few others signed up, the graduates in the room clapped and smiled too much. They said, "Congratulations, Linda," over and over again. Vicki and the other graduates who'd brought a guest entered the room. Vicki's enthusiasm made me nervous. She acted like we'd both won the lottery.

I didn't know what to expect from the training, but I

had nothing to lose. At the very least, maybe I'd discover what to do about my situation with Ordway.

Later that night, I realized I'd left my mink hat in the Mohegan. I'd bought it to go with the coat Ordway had given me for Christmas. The next day, I called the hotel's lost and found. There was no sign of the hat. Had one of those enlightened est people stolen it?

\*\*\*

The entire first day and night of the training was about rules. No talking to anyone in the room except the trainer or an assistant. If you wanted to ask a question or share something you were to raise your hand and the trainer would call on you. No leaving the room for any reason until bathroom or meal breaks were announced. If you had to go, too bad, you would not be let out. Ordway would have had a nervous breakdown trapped in the est training.

Like robots, the volunteers showed no emotion as they raced up and down the aisles with microphones.

"What if I have to change a tampon?" asked one young woman.

"You can't leave until bathroom breaks are announced," said Ronnie, the trainer.

"What if I have an accident?"

"You'll have to create it so that that doesn't happen, won't you?"

The woman's mouth dropped open.

"You people need to get it. You create your own reality."

Whenever anyone stood up to ask a question or share, we had to acknowledge them by applauding. Not sharing was frowned upon. "Don't try to hide. At some point I'll call on each one of you," said Ronnie.

We couldn't sit next to someone we knew; and the people on medication who'd had to show a note from their doctor, proving they needed the meds, had to sit in the back row so assistants could give them their pills at the right time. If you broke a rule, you were kicked out with no refund.

I could hold off going to the bathroom for hours. I knew how to grip my bladder. And I didn't expect my period for another three weeks.

Deconstructing every example of what breaking the rules looked like took the entire day, although I had no watch to verify that and there were no windows to see if there was still light outside. There were endless questions from people about what the rules meant. I stopped listening. When there was absolutely nothing left to say about rules, Ronnie asked for the hundredth time if there were any more questions about rules and sure enough there were. The man sitting next to me whispered, "Do you know when this is going to start?" *He's breaking a rule*, I thought. I whispered back, "I think this is it."

Ronnie, a stocky man with reddish hair, didn't talk. He yelled, in a loud, flat, monotone voice, like an Evangelical preacher but without emotion or enthusiasm. Periodically, for no apparent reason, his voice would become louder. My hands tingled and my heart pounded for fear I'd be called on for some kind of confrontation.

For no reason I could ascertain, he screamed that we were all assholes. I had no idea why or what he meant. But I had to agree that the people asking questions about rules for hours on end were assholes. He said he was screaming at our minds, that we were machines and we needed to get off it. Evidently, getting off it meant giving up a position of being right. "Most people would rather be dead than be willing to be wrong," Ronnie said. It was an enlightened being that got off a position, that put aside considerations and did things anyway. Wanting or not wanting to do something had nothing to do with enlightenment. Willingness to push through one's barriers and do the task no matter what was all that counted.

I welcomed his vocality. My early years spent moving with my mother and sister from one state, one father, one school to the next, without warning or explanation, had left me longing to hear the truth about the rage, sadness, and resentment my mother carried. Instead, she drank every night, sobbed in her bedroom before passing out, convinced that my sister and I never heard her sorrow or saw the devastation behind her fake daytime smile.

"You chose those parents you're so angry at," Ronnie yelled. "You assholes. You pretend you didn't choose them, but I know better. You're all fucking gods and you've forgotten. It's time to start telling the truth about that."

Complaining about our lives was a racket, and we were getting a pay-off for things being the way they were. But it was also costing us. In the training, we would learn about our racket, the pay-off, and the cost.

I wasn't sure how or why I'd created an alcoholic party-girl, sex-addicted mother, her four husbands—bad choices all, and my sister's stroke. The trainer asked others what they got out of creating being adopted or abused or incested or whatever. Mostly, he said, people came up with things so they could get sympathy or have an excuse for their failures. What benefit had I gotten out of creating my second step-father to steal my mother's inheritance and my sister's and my trust funds? So I would feel justified stealing money from a wealthy man? It would have been easier to live off my own funds, the sum of which, according to my mother, would have provided a wealth of opportunities for my sister and me. I never knew exactly how much there was. My mother told us our grandfather was worth "a few million" when he died.

Ronnie said we didn't have to understand the reasons— we only needed to accept that we had created everything. Why would I be so stupid to create such trauma for myself? I'd had to cultivate stoicism, and I was so skilled at telling darkly humored anecdotes about my childhood I'd been told I should be a stand-up comic.

But if I'd created my life exactly as it was, maybe I could change it. If I remembered I was god in my universe, which is what the training was designed for, my life would transform effortlessly. I'd chosen everything, so how could I be a victim? We'd forgotten we were gods, and we made an agreement to come and be in the physical world; part of that agreement was to forget who we were.

"You remind me of stuck windmills. We've got to get your blades moving so you can experience a process of transmutation from one state to a higher state, like a windmill transforms wind energy into electricity."

Every half hour or so, Ronnie would pick up a tall cylindrical stainless steel drinking cup with a screw on lid. Initially, I thought it was a martini shaker. He'd take the lid off and begin dramatically sipping and pacing around the stage, repeating in a loud voice what we'd already heard, "You create your own reality, you're responsible for it all. Most people would rather be dead right than be willing to be wrong. It's an enlightened being who is willing to get off it." He'd replace the lid, remove it again, sip more, and pace, never interrupting what he was saying. He'd repeat this process a few times and then put the cup back on the podium. His movements were like a choreographed dance, as if drinking from the silver cup had something to do with the hypnotic delivery of the training.

Was it tea, coffee, or some kind of speed to keep him going? We'd been told the training could go on for sixteen hours or more without a break.

At various times, assistants would deliver notes to Ronnie. He'd stop what he was saying, read the note, fold it up, put it on the podium, and continue talking. Other times, he would write something on it and hand it back, or he'd say yes or no or whisper to the assistant.

The special cup, the machine-like yelling, the pacing, the notes, the jargon—were these rituals of a secret society, a special esoteric club? I wanted to join. I wanted a mug and private notes.

In a room with 299 others, people began to reveal secrets they'd kept hidden for years. Were some of them planted there to tell stories to get the party started? One woman said she'd been a prostitute for five years, and only now did she see that she was responsible for creating her job and hating it. Everyone clapped. Did that mean she was going to like it from now on, or that she would quit? I wondered if she knew Ordway.

We did longer versions of the happy/sad processes I'd done in the guest seminar, and a new one where groups of us went on stage and faced each other, standing in two rows a few feet apart, and stared. If we looked away from one another or showed any emotion, the trainer or an assistant would scream, "This is an opportunity to go through your barriers without running your racket." People laughed hysterically, broke down sobbing, fell to the ground. One man fainted. The woman across from me stared into my eyes with so much kindness, a layer of my stoicism melted. Suddenly vulnerable, my armor of protection pierced, I wanted to bolt from the room. I couldn't stop crying until Ronnie ended the exercise, and I went back to my seat.

After we completed the "stare down" process, I took a deep breath and raised my hand. An assistant raced down the aisle. My skirt stuck to the back of my thighs as I stood up and clutched the microphone. I had to pee; there hadn't been a bathroom break, and my stomach burned from lack of food.

"Do we create feelings too?" I asked. "I've always had these feelings I can't name. I don't know where they come from, and they won't go away."

"Your feelings are running you," said Ronnie. "Shock and loss are the two feelings experienced at birth. Any feeling you have after that plugs into that memory, and you have a reactive machine-like response to one or both of those. Feelings don't mean anything. Just like your thoughts. You acknowledge what they say and you go on."

"I haven't told anyone this before, but I've been stealing money from my employer. I want to stop, but I can't give it up."

"You've taken the first step. You told the truth. Now you need to tell your employer," said Ronnie.

"I might end up in jail."

"Stealing is a crime. But it's the only way. Your integrity is out. That's why your life doesn't work. Get it?"

"Thank you," I said and started to sit down.

"Don't sit down," he yelled. "I know your mind is going crazy. It's your machinery. Do you get why you have to tell on yourself?"

"Yes, I get it."

"Why?"

"So I can't get away with it anymore?"

The room exploded with applause. Dizzy, I sat down. Sweat dripped from all parts of my body, ruining the vintage Chinese silk jacket my grandmother wore in Hawaii in the '40s and had given me to wear in New York. I put my head between my legs. I had to tell Ordway. It was the only way to be free of my stealing addiction. I was a criminal.

Towards the end of the training, I had no idea what happened, but I burst out laughing with everyone in the room, like we'd collectively gotten a cosmic joke. But what was it? I hadn't laughed like that since the acid trips I took in high school. My mind had stopped. What relief. I had no thoughts, no emotions, no guilt. Survival fears were gone. My solar plexus, now open and breathing, was no longer a black hole of unresolved feelings I had to numb. How long would this last?

After every person in the room "got it"—I still didn't know exactly what that meant and I supposed Ronnie could tell by the laughing—he told us he'd chosen to be a trainer so he could clean up his karma. "By serving one who serves," he said. "That's Werner."

In my state of euphoria, I vowed to clean up my karma too.

On the last night of the training, former graduates came into the room and applauded as we filed out of the ball-room. There was Vicki, smiling and winking at me.

\*\*\*

I went back to work and confessed to Ordway, starting off by saying that sometimes if there was petty cash left at the end of the week, I'd buy myself a steak and I thought it best if I left the job. I was prepared to say more, but he interrupted me.

"Well, I expected you to be honest, but you don't have to leave. We'll keep better track of the money."

But I'd decided my true calling was to serve Werner. I wanted to be part of transforming the world. I wasn't sure what that meant, but I concluded it had to do with relieving suffering. The est office said the next step was to take one of their graduate seminars.

I signed up for one called "Be Here Now." The series offered the opportunity to begin experiencing life totally in present time, with nothing added and without the constant "chatter-chatter-chatter" of the mind. *It's What's Up "Now" That Counts*, said the flyer. *What is, is; and what isn't, isn't. In this moment of now, all is exactly as it is, and as it isn't, and it can be no other way. This is one definition of perfect.*

"Be Here Now" was about "Be, Do, Have" and the faster one could go through that process, the better. If one could be totally in the present, the "Do" and "Have" would naturally flow one into the other. Therein lay the promise of acquiring everything one desired.

"What is, is." "Choose what you've got." "Choose where you are now."

At the end of the seminar, which was mostly a repeat of the processes and rhetoric of the training with the same no-mind results, we were schooled about how to enroll our friends and family in the training. We were reminded again and again of Werner's quote, "If you're not sharing it, you never got it."

I agreed. When I was excited about something that had helped me, I wanted to tell everyone. The recounting recapitulated the experience.

The seminar leader told the group there were cards under our seats and if anyone was interested in joining the est staff, they should fill one out, give it to an assistant in the back of the room, and someone would call.

\*\*\*

I went to the est office for an interview. It was in a very small space on the first floor of an old brownstone in the Village. There were so many people jammed into the space I couldn't imagine how they got anything done. It was crazy and hectic but looked like fun, everyone laughing and being "on purpose," pulling together to do an impossible job— transform the world.

I met with Rick, the new manager of the New York est office from San Francisco, a short, redheaded, chubby Jewish guy in heeled cowboy boots, who played with his bristly moustache when he talked. He told me since I hadn't done any assisting at est, I had no idea what I was getting into, and I needed to volunteer for two weeks before I decided for sure I wanted to go on staff. He introduced me to Kelly, an ex-prima ballerina, who'd just transferred to the New York office from San Francisco. She'd been working for est for a couple of years. I could tell she'd been thin at one time. Now, she looked like a ballerina who'd been stuffed like an olive, with a small head, drab blonde hair, pale skin that flushed easily, huge, buggy, blue eyes, and the dancer walk—feet and legs splayed apart, walking not straight ahead but as if she were going around something. She'd given up a thriving career with the San Francisco Ballet to work for Werner.

"After so many years of training, how could you give it up?" I asked.

"Certainty that my true purpose in life is to clear myself and the planet of limiting belief systems."

"Don't you miss dancing?"

"I don't have time. The applause I used to crave doesn't hold a candle to seeing the happiness on peoples faces after they graduate from the training."

"I admire your commitment," I said. I would've liked to see her on stage, ballet thin, the star, wowing audiences with her talent. I imagined her fans missed her.

Rick appointed Kelly as my mentor for my two weeks of assisting. We became fast friends, although when she asked me at the last minute if I was willing to fill one of the cashier jobs at a seminar one night and I said no, she blew up. "You're going to have to be willing to do whatever it takes to get the job done if you want to be on staff." I got it and did the cashiering that night. I had to remember that not wanting to do something had nothing to do with choosing not to do it. Willingness and doingness were all that mattered.

After two weeks, Kelly told Rick I was ready to go on staff. He agreed, but before he made it official, he wanted me to meet with Perry Pace, head of personnel for all the est centers, who was coming to town in a couple days.

Perry looked like a coiffed bookkeeper. He smelled of cologne and soap. His hair had been blown dry with amazing precision and sprayed to stiffness. He held his head forward, and his eyes bulged behind huge, thick glasses, seemingly searching for something outside himself to focus on.

I'd heard Werner had given him a new Mercedes, with a huge pink bow around it, a gift for "getting the job done." Maybe someday Werner would give me a gift.

There were rumors of other Werner gifts: mink coats—which I already had—expensive watches, and trips to Mexico.

"Are you willing to do anything to get the job done?" asked Perry.

"Of course," I said.

"Outrageousness, not reasonableness, is the name of the est game. The salary is seventy-five dollars a week. It's low because Werner wants to make sure no one is working for him for the money. The job is about serving."

"I've heard that Werner will sometimes pay for staff to go to a Rolfer or a chiropractor. I've been Rolfed and I'd like to have more sessions, especially when I feel stressed."

"The organization has gotten too big for us to offer those kinds of services anymore," Perry said.

"Oh."

"So, why should we hire you?"

"I've made a commitment to serve Werner."

"Lots of people have, and we don't hire them. They work as assistants for the opportunity to experience personal breakthroughs."

I couldn't think of anything profound. "I've been working as a secretary, and I can type really fast."

"There are lots of good typists. Why should we hire you?"

"Well, then, don't hire me," I said.

"You're hired."

Why had that been the right answer?

"Being on staff is for a lifetime unless you run into a barrier, some resistance you're not willing to get off of. Are you committed to getting the job done no matter what?"

"Absolutely."

A week before I went on staff, the office moved to a corporate building on the East Side. I was disappointed. I wanted to be in the Village.

\*\*\*

In September, Rick handed me an ochre-colored nametag, my name written in calligraphy, encased in plastic, and my est career in the enrollment department began. Why did he put me in enrollment? So far, I hadn't had much success in signing people up.

"Your main job," he said, "is to make sure Heather, head of enrollment, and your new boss, is in good shape because when she is, she's magic. And if you get the job done, I want you to know there's money in this game. And by the way," he said, his voice rising and flattening in tone. "You're much too attractive to dress the way you're dressed, and your hair's too short." I considered myself stylish except for the Birkenstocks I wore, having come down to the ground from six-inch platforms after getting Rolfed. I had on black parachute pants, a beige linen shirt, gray sweater, a thick black belt, and a red scarf. My hair was growing out from the short, spiky cut I'd had two months ago.

"I want you to look like that," Rick said, pointing to Heather. She was cute but her clothes were awful and her hair a mousy-brown, boring length. That day she wore a brown wool skirt, too big and too long, with a jacket to match, a beige polyester blouse, and thick burgundy-colored stacked heels, scuffed and worn down in the back.

Horrified, I said, "I don't have any clothes that like that."

"Figure it out," he said.

I used my credit card to buy ugly, boring est outfits. Kelly told me Werner didn't want anyone to stand out. Any barrier that would get in the way of someone signing up for the training had to be eliminated.

Kelly needed a place to live, and I could no longer afford my art deco apartment. We rented a place together two blocks from the office on the East Side near 42nd Street.

There wasn't a real kitchen, just a sink and a small refrigerator. I bought a hot plate.

In an attempt to destroy my old self and my sad history and begin anew, I tossed my photo albums and baby books down the garbage chute. A wave of regret welled up in my throat as they clanked down the long tube. I imagined them finding a home in Narnia.

Kelly said now that I was officially on staff, I should write a letter to Werner so he'd know who I was. "If you handwrite it, don't use brown ink with him or anyone else on staff. That's his color. He has a brown Mercedes. The license plate reads, SO WUT. If you type the letter, make sure you don't use the ten-pitch IBM Selectric that's in the office. That's what he uses. Don't sign it 'Love.' That's reserved for Werner too."

"You're kidding."

"No."

I supposed that made sense. There wouldn't be any confusion about who notes and memos came from.

"Oh, and if you want to write something private, put 'For your eyes only' on the envelope and no one else will read it."

I wrote in blue ink, acknowledged him for the contribution he was making, and said I was privileged to be part of it.

\*\*\*

Working in the enrollment department was the most dreaded, the most demanding burn-out job. Heather Spitz was known as a bitch—friendly one minute, mean, annoyed, or hateful the next. Things looked grim. One of Werner's famous quotes was, "You get what you resist. What you resist persists." I tried to surrender.

Heather told me I'd be responsible for recording all enrollment statistics and calling them into est central in San Francisco every morning as well as making charts with percentages and doing other kinds of math that I didn't understand. I told Heather that I'd flunked every math course I ever took from fourth grade on, so maybe it wasn't a good idea to put me in charge of calculating and keeping track of enrollment statistics. She glared at me, "Then it's perfect that you're responsible for the statistics being correct, and they'd better be correct."

The rest of my job required producing high enrollments at $250 a pop. I was responsible for how many people called in to sign up for the training (if no one was calling, I needed to "get off it" and create ringing phones.) I also had to schedule enough assistants to man the phones to answer those calls; train phone teams on what to say and how to fill out a registration card; and create high statistics for outgoing calls to people who'd attended a guest seminar, filled out a guest card, but hadn't registered for the training. Those calls were the toughest area in which to get good statistics. The people had already declined to register and were not expecting, nor did they want, a badgering call from est.

"How did you like the seminar? Did you get anything out of it for yourself?" said the phone script. No matter what the potential enrollee said, there was an answer. Most assistant phoners hated the job and weren't good at it unless they had a sales background. Assistants were assigned a job. They signed up for three to six months or longer for a minimum of three hours a week. Breakthroughs of enlightenment through service were promised, and many occurred—better relationships and more

happiness regardless of circumstances. Several unem-
ployed assistants worked in the office full time.

I also helped Heather manage the Guest Seminar Leader
Program (GSLP), which involved weekly meetings and
training sessions. I had to make sure the people who'd
signed up kept their agreements and showed up for all
training sessions. And I had to be a participant so I could
learn how to lead guest seminars. I set up the logistics
and filled special guest seminars for two to three hundred
people. These were led by a trainer and sometimes by
Werner. And I was responsible for setting and filling up
coffee hours—more intimate guest seminars held in graduates' homes. Graduates invited their family, close friends,
and neighbors. It took hours on the phone with the host
to make sure the environment was conducive to enrollment. People wanted to serve cocktails and have music.
Coffee hours were the testing ground for people who were
close to being certified as a guest seminar leader, so enrollments were usually low. Invariably, at the last minute, the
host would get nervous and want to back out, afraid their
friends would feel pressured and neighbors would think
they were weird. If a host felt particularly nervous, a staff
person, usually me, would get on the train to Philly to
calm down the host and lead the seminar and afterwards,
spend the night in a weird guest room under a smelly
bedspread with bad animal art on the walls.

Staff members were required to attend every training
graduation, which usually ended at two or three in the
morning. We whooped and clapped and handed out
pamphlets for the upcoming graduate seminars. The
trainees, some of whom I'd enrolled, were happy, uplifted,
and grateful. They hugged us with such enthusiasm my
ribs were sore by the time I went home.

I didn't know how I could possibly do so many jobs. There was no human way, but we were expected to be beyond human, like Werner. Heather wouldn't tell me how to do any of it. Did she know? When I asked for direction or instructions, she said, "Just create it so it all works."

Rick called Heather into his office every morning and screamed at her if enrollment statistics weren't high enough. Invariably, she'd then rage at me. Heather explained this was necessary for both of us, to get out of our minds, to "get off it," to be clear and create enrollments.

One morning, feeling desperate about how to calculate statistics—I'd taken to making up numbers, praying no one would notice—I envisioned a volunteer who would show up to do the job. That afternoon, Grant Benson came into the office and walked over to me, saying he wanted to volunteer in the enrollment department. He'd finished the training a week ago. He'd seen me there clapping for all the graduates. In those days, gay men were attracted to my androgyny. Grant was a math wiz. With Heather's permission, he took over doing enrollment statistics. "See, she said, "you can create your reality."

Grant loved doing math and working in the est office.

I'd manifested something out of nothing. In the past, I'd prayed, affirmed, chanted, and tried to will my desires into being, with little or no success. Now, with est, I was able to create exactly what I needed at least some of the time. My manifesting abilities could only improve.

The thrill was short lived. Getting the job done had nothing to do with manifesting assistants. It only meant getting high enrollment statistics. *Trying* didn't count, only results. I talked on the phone for hours without a break, alone or with my phone teams of six graduate volunteers. I got their energy up by leading them in a Broadway tune or screaming at their minds to get off it, like Rick had done with me. I led them in mock calls with resistant prospects so they could practice using their scripts.

"Did you hear anything at the guest seminar that made sense to you? And what was that?" we asked.

The excuses ranged from my husband won't let me, to my child is sick, to I don't have the money, or my mother just died.

"Have you stopped yourself from doing things in the past that you wanted to do? Is this a pattern in your life?"

The idea was to draw the person out, engage them in conversation about their life and enroll them in the training with the promise that whatever wasn't working could be fixed. We offered them their own unique transformation. If they didn't sign up, they didn't think much of themselves.

I began to feel bitter. A heavy shroud of failure and dread hung over me. Rick said it was my fault for not saying the right thing, for not getting off my shit. He decided to sit with me and act as my coach. He nodded or shook his head to things I said on the phone. After the phone team went home, I told him I wasn't a cheerleader. "You better learn how to be one because that's what this job is," he said.

Rick folded his arms across his thick chest, crossed his chubby thighs, and waved the silver toe of his three-inch black cowboy boot up and down near my leg.

"If you're clear, people will sign up. It's the natural order of things. You are here to get their considerations so they can get off it and sign up." He stroked his prickly moustache. "Everyone wants what's available to them from the training and your shit is in the way."

I wanted to bolt. I missed working for Ordway.

"What's going on with you?" Rick asked.

"I don't want to be here. I don't like being under the gun."

"That comes up for everybody. You're plugged in. You don't believe people will sign up over the phone, right?"

"Maybe."

"You keep forgetting what you're doing. This isn't a bank job."

"It's drudgery."

"It's about transformation and making a difference. Remember? It wouldn't feel like drudgery if you were getting results."

I couldn't argue with that.

The best statistics one of the phone teams produced happened the night I left them alone. Was that the secret? What did I get off of? Had I had a breakthrough? I spent a couple hours at the Italian place across the street drinking coffee and eating pastries, chatting with the Sicilian owner, who thought est people were crazy. "Too friendly, smiling if they mean or not. Not normal in New York," he said.

Back at the office, the team was bursting with energy. They'd enrolled all but one of the people they'd called. A breakthrough. They couldn't wait to see if they could do it again. Their eyes shined with renewal and relief. Rick was right, drudgery had transformed into magic.

\*\*\*

One day, I went into an empty bathroom stall for a cigarette. Staff was forbidden to smoke. I checked for my non-existent period. It had been reduced to one pale red drop every month, and my body was bloating up like Kelly's. All the women on staff ate like birds but blew up and stopped having periods. The men grew less facial hair and didn't need to shave so often. They also got very thin no matter what they ate. I wondered if working for est caused some kind of hormonal shift.

I noticed a new look in my eyes. I'd seen it with other staff people. It reminded me of a raccoon, a steel band of intense energy across the eyes that could stare right through a person, full of warmth or coldness at any given moment.

Day and night were no longer distinguishable. I was living in between sleep and wakefulness. Life was one long day with no end.

Vicki called once, and I hardly remembered who she was. We'd known each other in a different time frame, a different reality. She'd been smart to simply take the training and go back to her life.

I lit a cigarette, lifted my legs, and rested my feet against the stall door in case someone recognized my shoes. My hand trembled, and the cigarette fell to the floor. I drowned it in the toilet as two women came in and stood at the sink. Through the stall crack, I saw they were two assistants.

One applied a sliver of pink lipstick to her thin mouth. "Guess who I was with last night?"

"Who?"

"Aaron."

"No."

"It was amazing. You should try it. Having sex with a seminar leader moves your consciousness to a higher level. Can you tell the difference in me? I'll never be the same."

"Imagine what it would be like to have sex with Werner."

"Oh, god." Her lipstick case clasped shut. She pressed her lips together, no mouth, and let out an orgasmic moan.

"We'd better get back. Do you smell smoke?"

After the first few hours of Rolfing, I had sex with my Rolfer. No one had ever touched me so deeply, physically, or emotionally. The intimacy of the work led me to naturally want to have sex with him. He didn't deter my desire, and I had more change in my body with subsequent sessions.

Having sex with Werner would probably have increased my ability to manifest for Werner and myself. That seemed like the ultimate enlightenment. If I could prove my value creating stellar enrollment statistics, I could move up from office cog to a position with more money and be closer to Werner.

I went back to the office. Rick was screaming about low statistics.

"Okay, everyone, there are too many no's. Into the conference room." All fifteen staff people converged to the back room to spend four hours listening to Richard Pryor tapes in order to shift our minds, to get off it. Triggered about our bad statistics, it took us at least two hours to start laughing at Pryor's jokes.

If statistics didn't go up after this, Rick would make us vacuum and dust the office, clean toilets in the bathroom, even though a cleaning crew came in every night.

During these distraction times, assistants ran the office. Not surprisingly, they got more enrollments than we did. They had nothing to lose.

\*\*\*

Kelly and I ate most of our meals at the McDonald's or the Italian place across the street. We didn't have time to cook, clean, or do laundry.

She'd been on staff in San Francisco, where Werner lived. "He has people doing everything for him," she said. "There's a man named Rob whose job is to follow Werner around, including into the bathroom, and write down every word he says."

"We should follow suit," I said. I suggested we hire someone to do our laundry, clean, and do errands.

"We can't afford it."

"Maybe we can."

I called Diane, the temp agent from Career Blazers, whom I'd worked for when I lived with David. She sent us Barry, a young gay dancer who'd just moved to New York from Kansas City, willing to work for almost nothing. Kelly and I split the cost out of our paltry paychecks for him to clean and do our laundry. Embarrassed about washing our lingerie, he asked that we put it in a dark lingerie wash bag so he couldn't see it. He said he didn't want to be rude by hanging it up so we'd come home after a long day to a bag of wet underwear sitting on top of the toilet seat.

\*\*\*

One morning over coffee and an Egg McMuffin at McDonald's, after we'd finished "sitting"—a twice a day zazen meditation designed to accelerate our enlightenment, now a requirement for est employees since Werner's visit to Japan—I asked Kelly if she'd had sex with a seminar leader or a trainer. Or Werner.

"No, but you could," she said. "He shouldn't be married in this lifetime. He and his wife don't live together. I could see him with you. You're his type. He likes tall, classy blondes or petite, dark-haired women. Bill, the head of the well-being department referees fights and has to flip a coin on the nights Werner is available to have sex with someone."

"Really."

"It's usually between Lila and Gretchen. They're both tall blondes. They still work a lot, but they make a lot more money than we do, and Werner gives them expensive gifts."

"How can I make that happen? How do I meet him?"

"Oh, you will. The best way to be around him is to work in the est office in San Francisco. He's there all the time. You can manifest anything if your intention is strong enough. I'll help you."

That night after "sitting" again in a chair with our arms and legs unfolded, gazing at the floor—oftentimes, Kelly would get up and vomit—we lit candles on the wicker trunk we used as a coffee table. In the center, we created a game board with two little exhibits, one for New York, one for San Francisco. Each critical staff person became a cookie, a coin, a toothpick, or a match. Werner was the antique gold thimble my grandmother had given me. Since Kelly knew all the staff people, she chose their pieces and named them.

In order for me to be transferred, we had to figure out who would take my place in New York, and who would have to leave San Francisco.

Night after night, we tried out different combinations of toothpick, coin, cookie, and matchstick people. The thought of being with Werner never left my mind.

Two weeks later, I got a call from Ordway. He wanted to meet me at The Plaza for a drink and dinner to show me his latest police badges. He was lonely, and I knew that not too many people cared about those badges.

Hungry for an expensive meal, I agreed. I walked into the Oak Room Bar and almost passed out. There was Werner sitting by himself at the bar. I felt a surge of manifesting power. High intentioned evenings at the game board were manifesting. I was creating my reality of being near Werner, and I hadn't even gotten to San Francisco yet. I approached him and introduced myself.

"Yes, of course, Linda. Rick has told me about you." He took my hand in both of his. "Please, have a seat. What would you like?"

"Scotch and water."

I was irresistibly drawn to his penetrating eyes, aristocratic face, taut body, and powerful charisma that hinted of a dark side. I couldn't help but notice the barely visible pockmarks on his face. That flaw made him all the more attractive.

"How are the statistics for the week?" he said.

I had hoped for something more personal.

"They're pretty good right now, and our intention is to get them up with the five introductory seminars that are coming up." I could tell he liked that answer.

"How about dinner?"

My nerves raced every which way through my body. Here was my chance to get close to him.

"I'm meeting someone. Oh, here he is now," I said.

Ordway approached. I introduced them. Werner smiled and drummed his manicured nails on the bar. "Won't both of you join me for dinner?"

"We'd love to," I said. Ordway wasn't pleased. I stood up, and my mink coat dropped on the floor. Werner picked it up and motioned for the hostess to seat us at a table.

"She's eating with me," said Ordway.

"Maybe another time then," Werner said.

Ordway and I were seated. He laid out his badges in the usual leather cases, engraved with his initials in gold on the front. I kept my eyes on Werner. I wanted to have dinner with him. But I couldn't hurt Ordway's feelings. I owed him.

"Who was that guy?"

"My new boss."

"Oh. See this?" he said. "This is the biggest one so far. I had to get a special case made."

"That's nice," I said with fake animation in my voice.

"Do you like your new job?"

"Yes, I do."

"You can always come back to work for me. I'll never forget you."

\*\*\*

In November, Werner came to New York to lead a huge guest seminar at the Felt Forum. Heather and I had filled the place to full capacity. He invited the staff to a party upstairs after the event. I was eager to see him in action. He swaggered down the center aisle toward the stage at the Felt Forum, a cocksman with loose hips, long legs falling out in front of him, tipped pelvis, low-slung ass, dangling arms, and long, nervous fingers. Everyone stood and cheered. He opened with, "If God told you exactly what it was you were to do, you would do it no matter what it was. What you're doing is what God wants you to do. Be happy."

I wanted that.

Deafening applause.

"Might as well ride the horse in the direction it's going."

More applause.

He wore a slightly western beige suit with elbow patches. The edges of the lapels were stitched in brown. He looked one step up from a semi-slick car salesman from the west, making an attempt to look spiffy in New York. I guessed he was at the tail end of flimflam and moving into looking like a slick corporate guru. I hadn't noticed his clothes when I'd met him at The Plaza. Once he started talking in his loud, flat, mesmerizing voice about people realizing they were gods, I forgot about the suit. I couldn't take my eyes off him.

"What you call the universe is your universe. And there are a lot of your universes. The whole universe springs from the fact that you are. You don't need to do anything, say anything, prove anything. It just is. You don't have to work on it for it to be there. It comes from the fact that you are. And by the fact that you exist, my existence is. By the fact that I exist, you exist. And we are. We don't have to do anything to be with each other. We don't have to make our relationship work. We are related."

He was magic. He could sell anything to anyone, especially women. Even Barbara Walters looked transfixed during her interview with him that morning on *Today* as she unconsciously touched his thigh more than once.

Before he created est, he'd been the most successful used car salesman in Marin County. He'd sold encyclopedias door to door, and he trained his original est staff of three women to sell vitamins on the phone and in the streets of San Francisco as preparation for selling the training.

One of those women, Mari, had been a heroin addict in Haight-Ashbury. Werner cured her by putting her on the phones and holding her when she started to shake from wanting a fix. Then she'd go back to selling.

She'd come to New York with Werner to make sure the Felt Forum seminar was a success. She held a meeting for staff and assistants working in the enrollment department. She told a story about selling vitamins to an old man who had very little money. She said after a while it wasn't about vitamins, it was about selling the man on himself. His purchase meant a transformation had occurred.

"It's the same with the training. You're selling people on themselves," she said. "There isn't anyone that doesn't want that."

I commented on her beautiful leather jacket.

"A gift from Werner. For getting the job done," Mari said. I sensed they were lovers.

At the party, Werner took my hand in both of his as he'd done at The Plaza, stared into my eyes, and showed his big, white, even teeth. The edges of my skin melted. I lost my separateness. Those dark bullet eyes bored into me. His force field of energy threw me off balance.

"She's another powerful one," Heather said, standing next to us.

"Oh, I know. I met her before," said Werner.

He turned to the man standing at his left. "Frank Rawlins," he said. "My sidekick in enlightenment." Both men laughed. "He'll get you a drink."

"Hi there," Frank said as his drink sloshed around, almost spilling onto the floor. He was fiftyish with a full head of white hair and a face lined with thin, broken capillaries. He could've been one of my mother's alcoholic, gambling, salesman husbands.

He motioned for Heather and me to come closer. "How would you girls like to meet us later? We'll pick you up in the limo on the corner of 35th and 5th at midnight."

"Sure," we said in unison, standing by the food table.

Heather stuffed her mouth with raw zucchini.

"Does that mean Werner?" I asked her later when the men walked away. "Cause if 'us' includes Rick, I'm not interested. He's such an asshole."

"I think it's only Werner and Frank," she said.

"I can't believe it. What about Mari?"

"I don't know. Go. I have to stay here and do all these statistics from the seminar, make sure they're accurate. Meet them and then call me from wherever you are and I'll catch up with you."

"I can't go alone." Kelly and I had been intending for something like this to happen, but the thought of being fucked by Werner scared the hell out of me.

"Don't worry," said Heather. "He must like you."

"Does he do this with all the women on staff?"

"Not that I know of."

At 11:45 I put on my mink coat. I took the elevator down to the street and walked into the chilly night. My mind went blank. Where was I was supposed to meet them? I'd lived in New York for three years. But nothing looked familiar. Walking up and down the block, I tried to get my bearings. What was happening? I pulled the collar of my coat over my freezing face. After an hour of numbing confusion, I took a bus home.

"I got lost," I said to Heather the next day. She was pissed. She said I'd ruined her chances as well as my own. What chances did she have in mind? The women in the office couldn't believe I'd blown it. How could I have gotten so confused? Now, I was back in the sweatshop of enlightenment.

"You weren't quite ready," said Kelly. "We'll have to create another chance for you to be with him. Ideally, you being transferred to San Francisco."

\*\*\*

In the middle of December, each staff person received a personal invitation from Werner, written in brown ink, to a New Year's Eve party at the Hyatt Regency in San Francisco and a New Year's Day brunch at Franklin House, Werner's townhouse, referred to by San Francisco staff as "office of the source." There would be a two-day staff meeting prior to the party and all our expenses would be paid.

At a meet and greet before the meeting, Rick, like a pimp, introduced us, the New York staff women, as "his girls."

"When they don't get the job done, I call them, 'fucking queens looking bad,'" he said and laughed. I wanted to kick his fat belly.

I sat next to Heather, third row from the front. Across the room, four women from the est center in Dallas with big hair and lots of make-up were polishing each other's nails a hot pink color. A few rows up, I spotted Pat Woodell, the actress who played Bobbi Jo Bradley on *Petticoat Junction*, sitting in the front row.

Werner winked at her as he walked on stage carrying a microphone. He'd come from the ballroom next door where he'd finished leading an eight-hour seminar for the trainers. Looking as if he'd just showered and put on the light blue shirt that appeared freshly ironed, he scanned the room, flashed his teeth, sat on a tall stool, and said, "I know that you know that I love you, what I want you to know is that I know you love me." The room burst into applause. He was forty and looked thirty. Did he ever perspire?

"I want to acknowledge each of you for your commitment. We could have a world free of hunger and war if people had an empowering experience of themselves. Without est, nothing on the planet will change." He stood up and paced the stage in a languid way, his movement incompatible with the intensity of his voice and message.

"Thank you for being front line soldiers in the fight for consciousness. Many are called. Few are chosen. To transform the world, we have to create agreement for est, to hit a critical mass, that hundredth monkey. I can't think of a better purpose for my life. Can you?"

He talked on and on in a flat, mesmerizing tone, an incantation that pulled me into his swirl of conviction, which washed away my dark, junky thoughts and confusion.

From the back of the room, a woman stood and asked Werner how he was able to keep going for so many hours and never tire. He laughed. "I've processed myself out so completely, I'm never at the effect of anything. I don't have to eat or sleep or use the bathroom unless I give in to those urges."

I didn't know much about Scientology but it was well known that Werner had spent time processing himself with an E-meter, a device used by Scientologists for clearing members' emotional states.

Kelly said there was a rumor Werner had reached the highest level in Scientology when you give your soul to the devil and L. Ron Hubbard and receive worldly success and power in exchange.

"Too weird to believe," I said.

Werner called on a man in the front row who had raised his hand. "This is embarrassing and sounds crazy," the man said, "but I can't stop wondering if you are actually the Messiah."

People looked around the room at each other, unsure how to react; some rolled their eyes, others nodded in agreement, a couple of women cried and others laughed.

"No," said Werner with a straight face. "I am who sent him."

"Everyone who works for me, serves me," Werner said.

Many Muktananda followers worked for Werner but served Baba, as he was affectionately known. When his initiates became bored selling saris, tinkling bells, and other trinkets in the ashram gift shop in India, they had private meetings with Baba and asked him if they could work for Werner under the guise of serving him. He gave them his blessing, saying, "You'll be serving me." Werner wouldn't hire the women unless they cut their hair, shaved their legs and armpits, and put on dresses and pantyhose.

"What I want is for you to produce like the machines you are," Werner said. "I want est to work as efficiently as McDonald's. You have to be willing to do anything, whatever it takes for people to enroll in the training. Some people may get damaged in the process. What if I asked you to kill someone? If that's what it took to make the planet work. You couldn't do it. You're all too weak. You can hardly sit here for a few hours and stay conscious."

Kill someone? I squirmed. My ankles itched. I rummaged through my purse. Heather nudged me. "Pay attention."

"Sometimes the end justifies the means," Werner said. He scanned the room, side-to-side and front to back, acknowledging everyone. He snapped his head in my direction, and his eyes locked onto mine. I couldn't look away. He zapped me into some other reality. My thoughts and feelings disappeared. I don't know how long he bored into me. My body began to shake uncontrollably. *I've had some kind of mystical experience*, I thought. I was certain Werner was Jesus reincarnated.

Heather nudged me, "Do you know what happened?"

I shook my head.

She wrote *Shaktipat* on a piece of paper. "Your wick must have been very dry."

What was she talking about?

I continued to shake. I whispered, "Is he really Jesus?"

Werner went on talking. I tried to avoid his flashing jet eyes until the meeting ended.

Kelly pulled me close and put her arm around me. She led me upstairs to our room. In the clear glass elevator, I looked down into the courtyard. Plants and people and little round tables shifted in space as I rose higher and higher.

"This is weird. I can't stop shaking. I'm freezing cold. He gave me this look."

"I know. It's initiation. Shaktipat. It never happened to me, but I've heard about it. Werner received Shaktipat from Muktanada. Now he's a carrier of the energy. You're experiencing Jesus because he was a Shaktipat guru. Feeling cold with uncontrollable physical movement is normal."

"What is it?"

"It's when a recipient and the guru become one and the disciple wakes up. It can be done with a look or a hit to the body. It's meant to literally blow your mind and release Kundalini energy."

"So now he has total control over me?" I couldn't stop trembling.

Kelly helped me into a tub of hot water. The shaking subsided, at least on the outside of my body. Inside, my nervous system felt unhinged, unwired from how it was supposed to be, jumbled into a mess of frayed wires.

We only had an hour to get ready for Werner's New Year's Eve party. With Kelly's help, I put on make-up. Eyeliner and mascara intensified my glistening, piercing eyes. I wore the black and white flower print dress David had designed and made for me when we'd lived together.

By the time we went downstairs to the party, I felt fearless.

*\*\*\**

Whitish-gray smoke spiraled through the ballroom, softening the edges of the burgundy and black-striped wallpaper. Sandalwood, sage, and cigarette smoke wafted through the air. Werner, like a tribal king, wore a white silk suit, the see-through shirt underneath unbuttoned to his sternum. Thick leis of white and coral flowers encircled his neck. He smoked a fat cigar, leaving that smell and the scent of Pikaki at each table he greeted before joining his personal staff of twenty-five at a banquet table.

Didn't I deserve to be sitting there now that I'd been initiated with Shaktipat? I wanted one of two things: to be as close to Werner as possible or to be him.

Platters of food arrived at each table: saffron rice sprinkled with flowers, sushi, grilled steak, smoked duck, crab cakes, grilled salmon. The Champagne flowed.

The band played John Denver's song, "Looking for Space." The song was dedicated to Werner and had become the est theme song. After John took the training, he wanted to give up his singing career and work for est; but Werner wouldn't let him.

Specks of light spun from a big silver ball on the ceiling. Near midnight, Werner swaggered slowly to the stage. Like snowflakes, tiny blossoms drifted from his neck to the floor. The band stopped playing. He stood at the microphone. Silence filled the ballroom. He said the usual things about getting the job done and transforming the world in the New Year. Everyone applauded, and the lights went out. I moved close to the stage. At midnight, the band resumed playing, and the lights flashed on. Werner came down from the stage.

"Want to dance?" I asked. I penetrated his flower-laden chest and then his face with my eyes. Caught off guard, he danced with me for a minute. He moved with a stiff pelvis and legs like pipes. His swagger was gone. Obviously uncomfortable, he motioned for one of his cronies to come and take his place.

"Excuse me," I said to my unwanted partner and went to the bathroom. There was blood on the back of my dress. I'd started a full-blown period. An effect of Shaktipat? I was still reeling from what I perceived to be a mystical experience of Jesus in the form of Werner, although it was starting to wear off.

Back at the table, Kelly said, "I can't believe you asked him to dance. He'll remember you now."

"I don't care anymore. I want to figure out how he has so much power. At the party tomorrow, I'm going to copy everything he does: how he acts, how he is with people. Maybe I can pick it up by osmosis. Forget being one of his girlfriends."

\*\*\*

The next day, at the Franklin House New Year's Day brunch, I duplicated Werner's body movements, his actions, and his words. I tried to match his energy. I imagined myself as a magnet. I caught Werner watching me from a window seat in the living room as people crowded around him. If he zapped me again, I'd be ready for it.

After a while, I noticed people being drawn to me, wanting to talk to me. Before the party was over, I felt something important would happen—he would make a move toward me, ask me to come to San Francisco. Nothing happened.

That evening, I was on a plane back to New York, having thoughts of guns, pills, and jumping out the window of my apartment. I'd had a few drinks. Manifesting what I wanted hadn't worked. The same drudgery awaited me. My mind blurred. I fell asleep and dreamed of birds, road-runners, and ears of corn on the red rocks of Sedona.

*** 

Back at the sweatshop, Rick continued raging about low statistics. Shaktipat may have increased my aware-ness. Now I noticed a subtle smile on his face when he screamed, as if the yelling was a joke.

One day, he announced a new office policy, the arrival of Dr. Bob and the mandatory participation in the "About Sex" graduate seminar starting up the following week. He handed out charts we were to fill out and hand in at the end of the month with our daily "sitting" times recorded. If we missed a sitting time, showed up late, forgot our nametag, or failed to get the statistics we predicted, we would be fined one, five, ten, or fifty dollars, or another amount he would determine arbitrarily.

"When Dr. Bob comes to town next week, each of you will be assigned to do one or more sessions with him."

Dr. Bob was the director of the est well-being depart-ment. He'd given up his medical practice to work for Werner for seventy-five dollars a week. I assumed Dr. Bob was some type of therapist. Maybe he could help me clear what had held me back from my manifesting power.

I met him in a hotel room. The curtains were drawn. He introduced himself in a shy, soft voice and shook my hand. He removed the pillows and motioned for me to sit on the edge of the bed, facing the night table that held two tin cans wired to an odd looking device. He said the purpose of the session was to eliminate any barriers I had to being on staff.

"I'll ask you a series of questions while you hold the cans. If the needle inside this meter jumps then we'll clear the charge, the upset, or whatever emotional position you have about the question. Okay?"

This must be how Werner and other staff people had processed themselves out. That's why I had trouble with the job. I hadn't been sufficiently processed.

"Are you taking any drugs?" asked Dr. Bob.

"No."

"How about aspirin?"

"No."

"Are you smoking cigarettes or anything else?"

"No." I lied. I had been smoking.

I saw the needle spike, and he asked me several questions about how I felt about smoking. Was it something I wanted to do, did it make me feel good about myself, when I envisioned my perfect self, did that include smoking? After some minutes, I couldn't pay attention and the needle no longer moved.

"How do you feel about Werner?"

I told the truth about wanting to leave the job. "I feel conflicted. I want to help change the world, but the job is beyond exhausting."

"You know your life won't work until you eliminate these barriers and surrender to Werner."

"I guess," I said.

"Are you fucking anyone on staff?"

"No."

"What about Rick and other staff people? Who are they fucking?"

"I don't know," I said. I didn't tell him about Kathy who worked in the graduate department and Matt in accounting. The needle kept spiking so he kept asking. Finally, he moved on to another question.

Dr. Bob made notes, checked things on a list, watched the needle rise and fall. He grilled me for an hour until I had no idea what to say. Numb, with a blank, dizzy mind, I stood up.

"That was a start. I'll see you again next month."

He shook my hand, and I left.

At McDonald's, I stuffed myself with two burgers and an order of extra large fries.

How did people pass lie detector tests?

***

All staff members had to be enrolled in one graduate seminar (life improvement courses), another activity that took away personal time, but we didn't have to do anything in particular. We could sit back and get some rest.

The "About Sex" seminar was about clearing one's barriers to sexual expression and being willing to come from a place of ecstasy. Werner exuded sexual energy. That was his secret. No one could resist a pied piper.

"I'm deeply, completely in love with you," said the seminar leader, "and it's put me in a state of ecstasy, and all I want to do is share that experience with you today."

This guy didn't have an ounce of Werner's charisma or sexual energy and I couldn't imagine him in a state of ecstasy. I tuned him out and rested my eyes. An hour went by. Without warning, the room went dark. He said we were going to watch a birth film. A close-up image of a woman with her legs spread apart giving birth appeared on an enormous screen that took up the entire stage.

The room spun. I fainted. Two hours later, doubled over in my chair, I came to. Someone had pulled me to the back of the room. Soaking wet, dizzy, and nauseous, I sat up and asked an assistant what had happened. "You went into convulsions," she said.

"What?"

"Yeah, you were loud, making weird sounds, like a screaming hyena. Your whole body shook."

"What? How long did this go on?"

"A couple hours."

"For the entire seminar? Did anyone call 911? I'd say this was a medical emergency."

"We were told to let you be in your process."

I tried to stand. I stumbled and held onto the chair. I feared my equilibrium was permanently damaged.

*Fuck them all*, I thought. Nobody helped me as I left the ballroom, holding onto the walls to steady myself.

I took a cab home and went to bed. Unable to sleep, still reeling, I slid one leg out from under the covers and planted my foot on the floor to steady myself like my grandmother had taught me to do when I drank too much.

I remembered my mother's story of my birth. After thirty-six hours of labor, the doctor decided he had to pull me out with forceps. I'd read about the process. *Forceps resemble large salad tongs and are placed on the sides of the baby's head near the ears and cheeks. The doctor then gently pulls the baby's head downward during a contraction to guide the baby out of the birth canal.*

This description belied the violence of the procedure. I had red marks on my cheeks until age eight. I hadn't wanted to come out. I resisted being here. I must have physically re-experienced the trauma of my birth watching the film.

*I should see a doctor*, I thought. But est didn't provide health insurance.

***

The next morning, I woke to the sun streaming through my small but many-paned bedroom window. I went to the kitchen, my balance still wobbly, and put some eggs in a pot to boil, walked back to the bedroom, took off my pajamas, laid down on the floor, and positioned my pale, bloated, deprived body in a swath of sun that shone like gold on the hardwood. I fell asleep until a popping sound startled me awake. The over-cooked eggs had burst out of the now waterless pot. Six of them lay in tiny pieces on the floor. I turned off the hot plate, which was ready to explode, sat next to the eggs, and sobbed.

Fuck "sitting." I was already late for work.

Rick fined me fifty dollars. I explained what had happened the night before. But not feeling well was just a barrier to getting the job done.

"As of today, I'm giving you two weeks' notice," I said.

He took me into his office. "Whatever's going on with you will come up in your life anyway. You might as well deal with it here."

I had to get out.

"Once again, you've forgotten what this work is about."

I leaned out of the chair, lost my balance, and sat back down.

"You're an asshole," he said.

"Fuck you." The muscles in my legs that I'd endlessly bemoaned for their size, took over, lifted me out of the chair, and walked me out of the office.

Maybe nothing I ever did would be as important as transforming the world, but my body was certain it would never walk back in, no matter how my mind might justify returning.

Rick came to my apartment, talked through the door to convince me to come back. I wouldn't let him in. Later, he called. I answered the phone. For an hour, he made attempts to convince me to stay. No matter what he said, I repeated, "I'm not coming back. I'm not coming back."

Under a gray sky, I walked the streets every day, all day. My brain felt re-wired. People appeared alien in their black, somber coats and hats. Their eyes and lips looked as if they could drip off their faces. I'd seen this before coming off a bad acid trip years ago. No one smiled. No one understood what I said. I now only knew est speak. I'd been away too long.

As a child, I had a small plastic boat I floated in the swimming pool, imagining myself lost and alone at sea. I had paddles, a compass, and a map but didn't know how to use them. Nor did I know how to navigate the city anymore.

No one on staff would talk to me, the betrayer who would contaminate their minds.

Vicki, who'd gotten me into est, said she'd get me a job in advertising. "They've all taken the training. They'll hire you because you were on the est staff."

She introduced me to the head of the ad agency where she worked. He wanted to hire me on the spot. "I know you'll get the job done," he said.

"No, I won't." I walked out. I never wanted that kind of pressure again.

Kelly and I still lived together. She was disappointed the vision she'd had of me as a trainer was a bust.

"I don't have what it takes," I said.

"Oh, yes you do. I wish you'd talked to me that day instead of Rick. He's the asshole."

"How can all these other staff people do it, and I can't?"

"Oh, people on staff are always plugged in, up against the wall. It's normal. They quit and come back all the time. Eventually, they do enough processing and nothing bothers them."

"It's strange. I've gotten a few calls from graduates who were on my phone teams. They wanted me to know how much I'd contributed to their lives. I thought they hated me, I yelled at them so much."

"Sometimes yelling is necessary to break through someone's belief system."

"Thousands of people's lives have improved because of est. What's wrong with me?"

"You forgot what you were doing—making the world work."

"If only I could remember that, maybe I could go back."
"Ask Rick."

"Maybe you've learned your lesson," he said, but I don't have a lot of space for people who walk out. Write to Perry. If he says it's okay, I'll take you back."

\*\*\*

I flew to Phoenix.

I told my grandmother Werner had the same vacuuming standards she did and that I'd had to re-vacuum the est office and many ballrooms. "Like you taught me,"

I said, "slowly, laboriously, in perfect rows." She called him a "slave driver." *It takes one to know one*, I thought.

I wrote to Perry and waited. I moved in with my mother, painted her apartment walls Navajo White. I barely spoke. She chattered enough for both of us. I swam every day and baked my body in the sun.

Kimberly was living in a used trailer my mother had purchased for her after she fled from Bill, a Vietnam vet she was madly in love with. When he drank, he had war flashbacks and tried to hurt her. I called her a few times, but she didn't call back. One day, I went to see her, but she wouldn't open the door. Knowing she had a place of her own alleviated some of my distress over her continued misfortune.

I hated est, but I wanted to go back. I longed for it, like a lover. I'd had a purpose, been part of a family that shared a common goal. I'd been special, powerful, scared, and a piece of shit. The ordinary world was so boring. It occurred to me I might need deprogramming, but how did one find a deprogrammer? Weeks went by. I read *The Nature of Personal Reality* by Jane Roberts, a psychic who channeled an energy personality called Seth. She/Seth suggested that a philosophy or a belief system (and I would add a guru, a family member, or a step-father) with an insidious presentation could be more dangerous than outright lies. The kernels of truth in the mix could lead one to accept the distortions that are also part of it (or them).

I finally understood how I'd been seduced.

One day at the pool, a shy girl maybe ten or eleven visiting her grandparents, dog paddled through the water. "No, not like that. Kick your legs, reach out." Their voices carried noisily across the pool. Embarrassed, the girl froze, hung onto the stepladder, and cried.

I jumped in and swam from one end to the other. "Like that," the grandparents screamed, pointing at me. The next day, I went to the pool at the same time. They were there every day after that. The girl watched and copied me as I swam. A month later, at the end of her visit, she knew what to do. I watched the transformation in action—she pointed her toes, kicked her legs straight up and down, reached one arm out, then the other, slicing through the water like a windmill.

# A Small, New Life

After a year of living with my mother, I decided to study at the Rolf Institute in Boulder, Colorado. My body had walked me out of the est cult and swum me to a semblance of mental stability.

One day, while packing boxes, I found an old black and white photograph of my mother and me sitting poolside under a striped umbrella. I must be seven or eight. She wears fat sunglasses, an Esther Williams style two-piece with a halter-top. I'm in a shirred one-piece with tiny flowers. We're holding an open book. She's bent toward me, mouth open, eyes wide, her finger on a page. I look curious.

She was hopeful then, only on her second husband and still had her inheritance. I have a memory of her reading to me with animated expressions. I can smell the book and hear her voice. There's another photograph from the same time period of Kimberly and me laughing and jumping off a diving board together.

Later that morning, while swimming, I cried, remembering the day my mother taught me the butterfly stroke. My arms plunged through the water with the strength of a salmon swimming upstream.

It turned out I didn't have the body for Rolfing. I was too tall for bending over tables and my long, slender fingers couldn't deliver the amount of pressure needed to move peoples' thick, dense tissue and muscle into a better posture. I entered the Rolfing Movement program, where I learned how to move in a softer, more internal way.

I met Ben there, who was training to be a Rolfer. We had an affair during our three month training period. Afterwards, I went to Orange County with him and moved into his small two-bedroom apartment in Costa Mesa. He started his Rolfing practice in the back bedroom.

We came from very different backgrounds. He'd been born in Germany after the war—his parents had survived—and he came to the states with them as a child. A year later, we got married at the Orange County Courthouse and didn't tell our families. Neither of us could imagine his Holocaust survivor relatives who spoke Yiddish with suspicious looks when I was around and my much-divorced, highly critical, wasp mother who drank too much, in the same room together. So, we lifted our faces up to the thin, gray-haired court clerk dressed in a lime-green pantsuit and said our vows, holding hands on top of the beige Formica countertop while my married friends Nicole and Don looked on. Afterward, we had a Champagne brunch at an Italian restaurant in Newport Beach that I can't remember the name of. We had no money for a honeymoon. He went back to work the next day.

Ben stopped smoking when I did to make it easier for me. He knew everything about California wine and he made Zabaglione and Tarte Tatin from scratch. And even though he had never had a Christmas tree until he met me, he strung the lights more aesthetically than any

Christian I ever knew. No one before him had called me sweetie and honey, except my grandmother. He taught me how to read maps, buy electronics, and suck the meat out of chicken bones. On my birthday he'd give me a gift and then secretly hide another somewhere in the house. I'd discover it later and be taken by surprise like a child finding unsuspected evidence of love.

We argued about money from the beginning. We'd sit in the car outside in the parking lot of a grocery store, sometimes for hours, before we went in to shop, fighting about how much money to spend. I tried to tell myself we were balancing each other out, coming to some kind of middle ground, so we could stay together. I had to convince him to throw out the salmon-colored suit he wore to his cousin's wedding twenty years ago; and I told him if he wanted to be successful in Orange County, he had to stop Rolfing people from the back bedroom, dressed in yoga pants and old T-shirts. Eventually, outside the market, we'd come to an agreement somewhere between filet mignon and a can of black beans.

The marriage lasted ten years. The edges began to fray after seven.

I wasn't sure if he was already fucking Bettina when he informed me he wanted a divorce. It might have been after because that's when he started jogging again, which he hadn't done in ten years, and sunning himself from a lounge chair on the front deck of the house we'd recently bought and remodeled, wearing a faded black Speedo. His skin was too sensitive for sunbathing. He perspired easily like pale-skinned people from the north who'd rarely been tan. But now it was important to force some color into his skin, especially the white mark on his left ring finger.

There were sightings of my husband around town with

his girlfriend: at the Zinc Café, the Fahrenheit 451 book-store—where five of my paintings hung (had he pointed them out to her?), the Volvo dealership looking at new cars, walking the boardwalk at the beach, and Nord-strom—where my friends Julie and Vince saw them trying to hide behind the Lancôme perfume counter. Before me, my husband knew nothing about perfume.

When I told him I knew about his girlfriend, he said, "I don't know what I'm doing," as if he was talking to himself. He didn't look at me. He sat at the dining table, leaned way back on the chair legs with a guilty look, half smiling. I wanted him to fall backwards.

I finally decided to give up the house. My attorney had told me not to leave until I knew whether or not I wanted to keep it. Squatter's rights or something. We'd been living in separate bedrooms. I stayed in my room until he left for work in the morning.

At night, I shoved a beach towel in the space between the floor and the door, slept with a box fan blowing on high, locked inside what used to be our bedroom. The towel and the noisy fan blotted out sounds so I wouldn't stay awake all night waiting and listening for him. I didn't know until morning whether he'd spent the night with Bettina.

If he did come home, I waited in my room with the door locked until he left for work. He'd raged before, never hit me, but I'd started to feel afraid of him. I could sense his whole body wanting to be rid of me. If he got close enough, he might strike out with his hands, as unbendable as wooden shoes, dense from years of Rolfing people. The night he told me he wanted a divorce, he said if he'd paid attention to his intuition, he never would have married me.

One morning, missing him, I tiptoed down the hall, watched him get dressed through a crack in the door. His strong, stocky legs stood out from beneath his shirt. His black bikini underwear peeked out from the bottom of his shirttail. He looked toward the door and called out, "Is that you? What are you doing?"

I hurried back down the hallway. When I thought he'd left, I went to the living room. He startled me, said, "Hi, honey," like he'd said every morning since we'd been together. He'd forgotten what was happening. "Oh, sorry." He grabbed his briefcase and walked out the front door.

When I told my friend, Anne, about the divorce, she invited me to visit her in Boulder, Montana. I could stay at Boulder Hot Springs, the hundred-year-old hotel she was remodeling and turning into a bed and breakfast; soak in the mineral waters; take time in nature; paint; wait for my divorce to be final; and figure out what to do next. She told me Montana was like the Wild West, a great place to start over. Boulder was a tiny town, home of a tavern called "The Lounge," where in 1986 two drugged-up teenage boys shot and killed the parents of actor Patrick Duffy.

I'd never been to Montana, and from Anne's description, except for soaking in the mineral waters, had no desire to go. But I didn't have any other invitations, and I had to get out of Laguna Beach. I was worried about my health; I had heart palpitations, hip pain, and nausea.

I packed what I could fit in the Toyota, the newer car, which would be mine when the divorce was final. The burgundy interior still had a new smell. He'd had it hand-washed every week and waxed every two months.

The night before I left, we said goodbye standing behind the chairs at the Mexican pine dining table we'd just bought. He handed me receipts for some of the jewelry he'd given me: the gold charms, the marcasite watch, the Navajo earrings, the aquamarine and diamond heart-shaped ring, and the wedding band from Tiffany's. He said he had fifteen minutes before he had to leave for a basketball game. He wished me the best of everything, told me he loved me "in a way," and wanted to hug me. I shook my head, felt my collarbone sink into my chest. He put his right hand out as if he was completing a business deal.

\*\*\*

November was the worst time of year to move to Montana, where I would learn that car engines crack if you didn't heat them up, cats could freeze to death in front of your eyes, and no matter how many layers you wore or how much you turned up the heat, you had to take a hot bath most nights to get your bones warm enough to go to sleep. I was unfamiliar with snow that didn't stop at picturesque, below-zero temperatures and ice that didn't melt for weeks at a time. I'd never even been skiing.

I drove into the vast, sparsely populated, forbidding land with its big sky of droopy, tired clouds and highway signs for gun and quilt shows, and the "Merry Widow," "Free Enterprise" and "Lone Tree" health mines claiming that sitting eighty-five feet underground breathing radon gas would cure ailments ranging from tennis elbow to lupus. The idea of gassing oneself on purpose reminded me of the occasional and, since the break-up of my marriage, more frequent image I'd been having of putting my head in an oven à la Sylvia Plath.

Boulder Hot Springs looked like an abandoned convent where ghosts and vampires might hang out. In the 1800s, it housed a group of prostitutes who serviced Teddy

Roosevelt and other politicians of the day. They came to Boulder to hunt, drink, and soak in the mineral waters. A dilapidated bar still had liquor bottles from that time lined up on shelves in front of a cracked gold-leaf mirror.

Business was better than Anne expected, so I had to stay on the second floor of the un-renovated west wing, which had no heat and no working bathroom. She put thick quilts on the walls to make the room warmer. I slept in long underwear, two pairs of flannel pajamas, wool socks, gloves, and a knit cap pulled over my ears. Sometimes the temperature dropped to thirty below. The closest bathroom was down two flights of stairs and a long hallway. Anne provided a wide mouth thermos in case I had to pee in the middle of the night.

Because of a wiring fluke, the lights in the hallway of the west wing stayed on all the time. A bright rectangle of yellow shone around my bedroom door and reflected itself in the black sky outside my window. I kept thinking if that door in the sky would open, I'd find an image of my future.

Anne, a former therapist, had created an alternative to traditional psychotherapy. She didn't believe in antidepressants or in the interpretations made by therapists about what their client's had experienced in therapy. She called her system Living in Process. It involved peer support, allowing feelings to come up and processing them through the body.

One day I heard sobbing, wailing, and screaming. I went downstairs to the "process room," an old ballroom filled with mattresses on the floor. About fifteen people were on the mats, "having their feelings," as Anne said. She told me they were her trainees. They'd come for two weeks of instruction, to learn her unconventional method of how to deal with their emotional pain. "Abstinence from all addictions is a prerequisite," she said. It looked and sounded like, I imagined, primal therapy.

"What about the bed and breakfast guests?" I asked.

"The place is big enough that they never hear a thing. I bought it as a B&B and a training center. Do you want to try the deep process work?"

I realized this was the real reason Anne had invited me. I'd wanted to let myself fall apart for as long as I could remember, but until now hadn't been in the right environment. With the break-up of my marriage, I felt triggered all the time, constantly trying to choke down hundreds of heartbreaking memories. So I said yes.

Every day, from then on, I collapsed on a mat while someone sat with me. I sobbed so deeply, my bones creaked. I made loud growling sounds, pounded on stacked-up pillows until my knuckles bled. I'd start out screaming about my husband's betrayal, and in minutes, my mother, father, and step-fathers' abandonment would shoot through me. Day by day, I screamed in a primal way, curled into a fetal position. My skin got clammy as I processed through my childhood traumas: my mother's multiple marriages and divorces; terror of new fathers; sexual abuse; my damaged sister, my inability to save her, and my resentment that she'd taken most of my mother's attention since the day she was born.

I grieved too much for the clapboard Laguna Beach house with ocean views that I'd remodeled from a trashed halfway house for drug addicts. I longed for the new kitchen I'd designed on a computer at Home Depot; the ceramic knobs I'd obsessed about for the new glass and blond wood cabinets; the Berber carpeting; the plantation blinds; and the Malibu lights for the walkway I'd had to fight to spend money for.

At the hot springs, there were days of emotional calm when I could see that the marriage had been doomed from the start. I'd insisted on it, afraid that at thirty-three I was too old to continue just living with someone. Then I'd break down again thinking of our first date at Zeno's pizza parlor where I felt attracted but embarrassed to be seen with him, three inches shorter than I. *So shallow of me*, I'd thought. As time went on, I got over it. I decided his stocky build made him seem taller. He called me every day from work to tell me he loved me. He cared whether or not I had an orgasm. Soon after the marriage, incest and sexual abuse memories began to surface. Ben's safe touch must have been the very thing my unconscious had been waiting for. He paid for therapy but wouldn't go with me to the couple's group like other husbands. I didn't understand his passivity when I told him I'd caught the peeping tom from next door spying on me through the bathroom window. My throat tightened and my limbs trembled when I demanded he speak to the creep. "You have to stop him," I said. Why didn't he want to beat the guy up? Shouldn't he protect me? Was it his immigrant fear of an encounter with the police even though he had a green card? I didn't ask. He'd admitted to that once when we were stopped for speeding. He broke into a sweat when the cop approached the car. Reluctantly, he finally went next door. He wouldn't tell me what happened, but I didn't see the guy after that.

\*\*\*

One day, after nine months at the hot springs, the processing stopped. Anne said that would happen. I looked ten years younger, and I wasn't interested in Ben. I no longer hoped for a "come back home" note each month when I went to the post office to pick up my spousal support check, which he had to pay me for six more months.

I knew I'd leave Montana, but I didn't know where to go. Until I decided, I needed a place to live. I moved to a sprawling split-level, three-bedroom house on Jerome Place in Helena. The western artist who'd lived and died there painted downstairs in the red brick basement. The neighbor in back, whom I met one morning taking out the trash, told me Mr. Dickenson was a hell of an artist but never thanked anyone for anything. He recounted all the things he and the other neighbors had done for him over the years. He seemed especially resentful about the meals he and his wife had cooked and delivered to the grieving widower after Mrs. Dickenson passed away.

The couple I rented the house from bought it after Mr. Dickenson died. Dave was a journalist for the *Independent Record*, the local newspaper, and Crystal ran an antique store. She asked if I had anything antique or vintage from my divorce to put on consignment.

I set up a studio in Mr. Dickenson's windowless basement and went to work on a painting about my divorce, the final piece for a triptych, which would depict three stages of my relationship. I'd finished two of them at the hot springs. The first one, called "Dollin," was a collage made from Krazy Kat comics in the shape of a man and woman embracing. Before we were married, my husband read Krazy Kat comics to me. He'd pat the shabby futon in his studio apartment, signaling me to sit next to him. Then he'd read while running his sturdy thick finger along the strips. Some were drawn in black and white, others were painted in George Harriman's desert palette of yellow ochre, red oxide, sandy pink, and turquoise, where Krazy, Ignatz Mouse, and Offissa Pupp acted out their love triangle in the Desierto Pintada of Coconino County, Arizona. Every once in a while, Ben would look up and say, "Amazing!" and kiss me on the cheek.

The second piece I titled "La Boda de la Guera y el Judio" (The Wedding of the Blonde and the Jew). It sounded better in Spanish. I'd cut down our actual wedding clothes: his shirt, which had become a pajama top for me, and part of my dress. I glued them onto wood in the shape of bodies and made white masks for heads, painted their faces, covered one with a white veil. I finished this piece in a few hours and didn't stand back to look at it until the end. It turned out to be more disturbing than I imagined. The man had taken on a look of terror, and the woman, underneath the lace, a sad smile of resignation.

I worked on the third piece for two weeks but ended up painting over murky colors and nebulous images over and over again. I thought Mr. Dickenson's vibes, minus the western art aesthetic, would help. Maybe I didn't yet have enough distance.

I liked the yard, but it was too big for me to take care of. There were lilac bushes, a spruce and a pine tree in front, and beautiful pear and apple trees in back. I assumed Dave and Crystal would pay for a gardener, but they didn't want to spend the money. I hired a teenage boy to mow, but I had to water the front and back two or three times a week. It took hours to move the sprinkler around so it hit all sections of the grass evenly. There were still brown spots. It was a thankless job. My yard was the worst on the block. I couldn't keep up with the neighbors who all seemed to be around seventy. They must have been retired government workers because those are the only decent jobs in Helena. They lived for their lawns. They mowed, watered, trimmed, planted flowers, and pulled weeds almost every day. In winter, they shoveled snow each morning. I learned that most native Montanans were from Norwegian stock and they loved hard work. It seemed the harder something was to do, the more alive they felt. I did not relate.

In May, tiny pink blossoms scattered through the apple trees. Most days it was sunny, but not that warm. In the beginning of the month it snowed, which saved me two weeks of watering. It was never hot enough to sunbathe. I missed that.

Occasionally, in the early morning, two or more deer would come to the front yard. They'd lie down under the pine tree like dogs and sometimes come right up to the window and look me straight in the eye. The neighbors were curious about me too: a woman in her forties living alone in a three-bedroom house on a street with retired couples. The neighborhood streets were hilly. I walked an hour up and down them every day. I could feel eyes at the windows watching me.

A woman from across the street came to the front door one day. Standing as tall as my breasts, she handed me a plate of little yellow cupcakes to welcome me to the neighborhood. "To match the color of your house. They're made from scratch," she said. I knew I should have invited her in, told her all about myself, but I didn't. I said thank you, took the cupcakes, and closed the door. Later I noticed the plate wasn't paper. I'd have to return it and face another opportunity to reveal myself.

I couldn't tell the woman my plans because I didn't have any. I signed up for a computer class, thinking I ought to focus on learning marketable skills instead of painting. I couldn't concentrate. The class was filled with homeless people and women, shaky from recent withdrawal, who lived at a halfway house by the railroad tracks, hoping to get a job and a place of their own. I didn't go back.

Allowing my husband to support me financially, so I could do art, had been a mistake. I'd felt increasingly obliged to pay up, be cheerful when I wasn't, and have sex when I didn't want to. And though I sold many art pieces over the years, my income was not consistent.

***

Now I worked on my divorce painting and waited for a sign of where to go next. I couldn't take another winter in Montana. Snow was not beautiful to me. Stark white-ness on the ground meant ice. I was claustrophobic. Being cooped up for days on end waiting for it to melt made me anxious. The men here liked to drive their trucks on ice. I'd see pairs of them in the front seat laughing as they swerved and slipped on the roads. There were usually one or two large dogs sitting behind them, as if they were wives, and a bleeding, wide-eyed deer, dead or dying in the flatbed.

For years, I had wanted to live in L.A., a better place for an artist, but my husband wouldn't move. Now I was afraid to start over in a big city by myself. Laguna Beach was the least conservative place in Orange County. There were gay people and a few Democrats, but when I thought of the Sawdust Festival of bad art, three million tourists a year, countless galleries chock full of seascapes and blown glass ocean animals and the potential to be triggered again by memories of my husband, I couldn't imagine moving back there.

But I had to go once more to retrieve what I'd left behind—my artwork and half the household goods. My attorney talked to my husband, but he wouldn't send my things. She said to pick a day to move, and she'd arrange it so he wasn't at the house.

Laura was the only woman of the seven lawyers I had interviewed. I dressed up for every interview, high on too much coffee and multiple donuts. Did I still have the knack to attract a man? I tried flirting with the cute male attorneys. The predatory one—who had given me his card at an Alcoholics Anonymous meeting after I shared about getting a divorce—I didn't flirt with. I chose Laura and wondered if I'd ever have another relationship.

\*\*\*

The jasmine bush and the six-foot-tall stalks of sunflowers my sculptor friend, Gerard, and I had planted during the remodel had shriveled. We'd carefully wrapped the almost dead bush around the gray wooden fence hoping it would revive itself if it had room to spread out. Gerard planted Mexican sage, ice plants for ground cover and to help with erosion. The car noise on Bluebird Canyon Drive had increased. When we'd first moved in, I remembered thinking there was too much traffic to attract many birds. Sometimes they came early in the morning, but in the year I lived there, I never saw one single bluebird.

My paintings were stacked in groups against the walls in the living room. Maps of Orange County, secured with pushpins, hung in place of my art. There was Champagne in the refrigerator, jars of instant coffee with vanilla flavoring on the kitchen counter along with a row of knives neatly laid out: evidently what he considered my half. Mold in the back closet had grown and eaten my grandmother's vintage fox fur hat, and there was a smell of cheap body lotion in the bedroom.

There was a photo of a woman on the dresser. It had to be Bettina, standing in front of "Every Bloomin' Thing," her flower stand, she'd set up in the courtyard of his office building. That explains why, toward the end, he'd started bringing home so many bouquets of flowers. She looked ten years younger than I, definitely not in menopause. Her mouth was toothy, and she had a horsy face. Her head was cocked in a flirty, not smart way. I imagined the flower girl giving him as many blowjobs as he wanted and sitting with him through bad movies. I found receipts from the Quail Ridge Resort in Sedona where he'd taken her for a weekend—the same place we had stayed for our anniversary two years before. I looked through his closet at the suits and shoes I'd picked out, the cowboy hat from Santa Fe. I smelled his pale blue, lightly starched shirts.

I told the movers what to pack. I found a box of photos I hadn't had time to go through before I'd left. I made sure to leave him some particularly good ones of me. I put together a pile that were taken at his father's eightieth birthday party. I had worn a revealing jade green wool dress. My nails were painted with alternating pink and lime polish. I added the ones he took of me in Idyllwild sitting under the pine trees outside Kathie's Café wearing bright red lipstick and big black sunglasses, looking like a celebrity. I was sure he'd be sorry. I guessed I had more to process when I got back to Montana. There was a striking picture of him at the same café, with his strong square jaw in three-quarter profile, an almost imperceptible look of resentment in his eyes that I hadn't noticed before.

I wondered what Bettina did about the snoring. I'd tried sound machines, noisy fans, waking him up every time he woke me up. He'd ended up sleeping all over the house—on the couch in the living room, on a foam pad in the hallway, on the thin sofa bed in the den off the kitchen, listening to spinning refrigerator sounds, which he said reminded him of having to sleep on a cot in the kitchen as a child in Germany after the war.

I recalled the first time his hand felt oppressive and controlling on my thigh as he drove in that aggressive, annoying way. He'd been ignoring me, working sixteen hours a day, but pretending to be attentive. I moved his hand, said it was too hot. He tried again. I crossed my leg away from him. Eventually, he stopped reaching over.

He'd be coming home soon. He told Laura he'd stay away until eight. Before I left, I walked through each room trying to remember love, however fractured.

I stared into the bathroom mirror and thought of him bent over the sink, brushing his teeth after a shower, light reddish-brown freckles dotting the tops of his hands. His cuticles were thick. He peeled them sometimes. I remembered how I put my arms around his naked waist, smelled the side of his neck behind his ear, tugged the damp curls from the back of his scalp with my red painted nails and then touched him.

I'd taken my wedding ring off before I left for Montana. Sometimes there was still a phantom gold band from Tiffany's, inscribed with *Sweetie*, making an ache in my finger. I felt it now, quivering with regret as I put the keys on the kitchen counter.

That night I splurged, spent the night at the Surf and Sand resort down the street. I stayed awake all night with the windows open, smelling the ocean.

\*\*\*

Back in Montana, I waited for my things to arrive. I still didn't know where to go but in preparation, I held garage sales every weekend. I sold my jewelry, scarves and dresses, drawings and paintings, for too little money, and my record collection. Men asked me to show them the guns and ammo.

"Any knives?"

"No," I said.

"Tools?" I shook my head.

"I guess your husband wouldn't let you bring those out."

I finished the third part of the triptych. A painting in vibrant oranges and reds of a nude woman's back covered with words, markings, symbols, and lines of my poetry written in colored oil stick crayons.

I titled the piece "Private Graffiti" and sold it to a couple that came to my final garage sale. They said they collected art and were on the board of directors at the Holter Museum.

Soon after, on a day when thunder cracked, lightning flashed across the sky, the neighbor's dog jumped three feet and snow was predicted for the first week of September, I knew it was time to go.

The day I left, a group of deer gathered in the yard. They watched me as I drove away, my car piled high with my small, new life. I went south, stopped in Las Vegas, and spent the night at the Sahara where the three surviving Platters were singing in the lounge. I ate a steak dinner for $7.95. The next day, Tom Waits sang "Amazing Grace" on the radio as I hit L.A. from the 60 Freeway.

# Million Dollar Red

She's crazy! She's gone too far.

One day, we were sunbathing by the pool. I settled back in the turquoise, slatted lounge chair, spritzed my face and ankles—my poor, thin ankles were all cracked from the sun. The dermatologist said I was scorching myself, but the sun was the only thing that relaxed me. She squirted white lines of sunblock over her thighs and, out of nowhere, asked me if she'd ever been molested.

I was so shocked. Of course, I denied it.

She said she'd been having flashbacks of disembodied penises and dreams of being pinned under a man's body. Her therapist said it was probably one of my husbands. If that were true, I'd know about it. Kimberly never said anything.

Linda's never been happy. She was painfully shy. That was her problem. I had to arrange for boys to take her out. I always had boyfriends. Hundreds of them.

Bud was my first husband. His real name was Royal, but he was a junior so everyone called him Bud. He was the girls' father, although you'd never know it. He never paid a dime in child support.

The day I married him, I knew I'd made a mistake. On

our honeymoon we stopped in Greenwich Village and I wanted to stay there with all those Bohemian artists. I had studied speech and dramatics in college, had my own radio show for children, wrote the stories and did the voices myself.

Bud was the catch of the season, tall with blond hair, a genius at math, and he played terrific honky-tonk piano. All the girls in college went to bed with him. I wouldn't sleep with him, so he married me. Later, he had an affair with a floozy from Calumet City and on his way home one night, drunk, he killed a man in the road. Daddy got him off a manslaughter charge.

After our divorce, Bud married this woman, but she couldn't have any children. If I had it to do over, I wouldn't have any children either.

Linda is now doing paintings of naked people. She showed me photos. She said she started them one day after she had "a memory."

She said she hid from Ed, my second husband, in a playhouse in the backyard. He'd been coming into her room at night when she was asleep, pulling the covers back, slipping his hand into her pajamas. "It started when I had pink eye," she said, "when I had to keep my eyes closed with medication. Remember, Mother?"

Ed, of all people. He was very nice but not exactly a man of passion. The only reason I married him was because everyone thought he would make such a good father for the girls. Linda never liked him. She didn't like anybody. Later, Ed got the idea he should be a priest. It broke up our marriage, but does that sound like a child molester to you?

By the time I was thirty, I knew the right outfit for

divorce court: a tight navy blue suit, slightly sexy but not too much, pearls, white gloves, and a wide-brimmed hat.

Over the years, people have told me that I resemble Gail Storm, Peggy Lee, and Jackie Kennedy. I love "Million Dollar Red" lipstick. I have the polish too. I told my friend Cherry Arquilla, the original Chesterfield girl, and the rest of the girls in the models' guild that the legs are the last to go. Later, they all told me I was wrong. Well, mine are the last to go.

My third husband, Jack, wore black horn-rim glasses and had a squarish body. I married him the summer Linda turned ten, Kimberly eight. Jack and I cut our Las Vegas honeymoon short and drove to Buffalo Creek, Colorado to pick them up from summer camp. I could hardly wait to tell them my news.

"This is Jack," I said. "We just got married. You girls can call him Daddy." Kimberly liked him right away. All Linda said was, "Has he been in our house?" And then announced that she wouldn't call him anything.

And he was so nice, opening the car door for her, asking her questions about camp. I practically had to push her into the backseat.

I'll never forget breakfast that morning. The girls ordered blueberry pancakes. I needed a drink. Jack ordered Bloody Marys and Shirley Temples. He told the girls that when we got home he'd buy them a horse. Linda said, "It's not your home." So rude. It was a difficult summer, but Jack had the type of personality that little by little brought Linda out of her shell.

The first thing that really impressed her was the night we had trout for dinner at the fishing lodge. She was worried about choking on bones. Jack slit the fish open, pulled the whole skeleton out with every bone attached.

He bought the girls a trampoline and taught them how to dive. He paid for their braces. Kimberly had buckteeth. Linda didn't really need them but her mouth looked a little too pouty. Jack thought her mouth looked like Bridget Bardot's. Not true. She was much too flat-chested to look like Bridget Bardot, much smaller than I was at her age.

Jack wanted to legally adopt the girls. He was a big spender and a great cook. He covered quail and other small birds in delicious sauces, and when he barbecued hamburgers, his hands patted the meat as if he'd had a relationship with the animal that died for it. He was the most adventuresome man I'd ever met. He didn't have a regular job. He made money by making produce deals and betting on sports games over the telephone.

Jack was always making me laugh, but I found out he had a gambling problem. He bought me a pink Cadillac convertible. He didn't have the money to pay for it. I was flattered but felt uneasy. Everything was on credit. He bought the horse named Honeybee that he never completely paid for either. The girls took very expensive riding lessons. Jack was terrific when he had money. When he didn't, he pretended he did.

He stole the inheritance money I got when Daddy died, plus the girls' trust funds. I don't know how he got away with forging my signature. He lost all the money on a bad crop of cucumbers in Salinas.

He was so upset after I asked for a divorce that he came to the door one night with a gun. He broke it down and threw a head of lettuce in my face. Linda had to call the police. He left before the police came. They asked all kinds of questions. "Was he drunk? Are you still married? Did he hit the girl? Did he hit you?"

"With the lettuce," I said. "I want a restraining order."

The whole time they were there, Andy Williams was singing "The Hawaiian Wedding Song" over and over. It was stuck on the record player. Later, Jack sent me the record "Stranger on the Shore" to let me know that that was how he felt. If it hadn't been for the girls, I probably would have stayed with him.

Linda has made up stories about Jack too, with the help of her therapist. These people are making a fortune planting incest ideas in the minds of people who can't remember their childhoods. What is the point of dredging these things up, anyway?

She said that when I used to travel with the model's guild, Jack came into her room at night and tried to get in bed with her. I told her that if that's all that happened, it wasn't so unusual. Daddy used to do the same with me when he'd had too much to drink and got confused about whose bedroom he was in. Certain things run in families, like diabetes.

Linda said Jack paraded around naked in the laundry room when he changed into his bathing suit. When I wasn't home, he'd stand in the doorway of her bedroom and watch her get dressed. Lies. I asked her why she didn't just close the door. She said it was no secret that Jack and I had a troubled sex life. She used to hear things through her bedroom wall. Well, it was just the opposite. We had a terrific sex life.

I can't get her to stop telling these lies.

Kimberly doesn't remember any of this.

Later, Jack was killed. He was drunk and got thrown from a horse. Hit his head on a rock and cracked his skull right open.

I've been so disappointed with men.

I was a divorcée for seven years, and it almost killed me.

My nerves were shot. I had to take double the amount of Dexemil for my pre-menstrual tension and go to work for the first time in my life.

We had to get out of town; Jack had run up so many bills. We moved to Florida. I didn't know anyone there except my cousin, Jimmie, who lived in Fort Lauderdale. He promised to help me out financially.

Jimmie thought of himself as a jet setter. He owned an airplane, called himself Colonel when he wanted to impress people. I hadn't seen him since college. He still talked out of the side of his mouth like Humphrey Bogart. In school, all the girls thought that was so sexy.

Well, he talks that way because when he was a child, his mother used to hit him across the face with a belt. She even tried to abort him by taking quinine pills when she was six months pregnant. And his side of the family always thought they were above us!

Jimmie found us a house to rent on a canal. He invited the girls to go out snorkeling on his boat one Saturday with his five children. Kimberly was sick so Linda went by herself. I spent the last of my savings on a bikini, a white lace cover-up, and new thongs for her. Her stomach was too white. I tried to get her to use Q-T Quick Tanning Lotion but she wouldn't, and she insisted on wearing that ridiculous Tiki god around her neck.

I took his invitation as a good sign. He was including us in a family event. So far, there had been no offerings of money, only vague invitations to someday visit his house in the Bahamas.

Linda came home sunburned and with cuts on her legs from coral. I don't know what happened out on that boat, but Jimmie didn't call after that. I asked her if she'd done anything to upset him. She wouldn't say a word.

A month later, he called and invited me to a party at the Palm Bay Club in West Palm Beach.

The next morning, Kimberly accused me of "fucking" Jimmie on the living room floor, said she'd gotten out of bed for a glass of water and saw us and a fifty-dollar bill on top of the wig I wore to work.

Well, Kimberly was being influenced by her girlfriend's mother who told her that when women get divorced they get real horny (a vile expression). I told her that was just ignorant talk. This was one of the problems with having to live in a lower-class neighborhood.

I did have a lot to drink that night. I remember eating sand dabs. And at some point, I think we went swimming, somewhere. Oh, I don't know. What makes the difference? I never saw Jimmie after that. He obviously had no intention of helping me.

I got a job at Saks Fifth Avenue in the Better Dress Salon. The girls worked there too, on Saturdays and during the Christmas holidays, wrapping gifts and selling men's cologne.

We moved to a small apartment in Pompano Beach. I could have lowered my expenses by sharing a place with another divorced mother, but I didn't want to subject the girls to strange men who might be sneaking around at all hours.

Daddy would have rolled over in his grave if he could have seen us having to struggle.

I had no choice but to send Linda back to Phoenix to live with her grandmother who wouldn't send me a lousy hundred for a car payment. She wrote letters telling me the way to save money was to do all the ironing at one time.

Daddy was right. On his deathbed he said, "Your mother has no heart."

Eventually, I went back to Phoenix and met Carl. When I told Linda I was going to marry him, she said, "Who the fuck do you think you are, Mother, Elizabeth Taylor?"

What a thing to say to your mother!

Carl and I got married for tax reasons, plus he was so good in bed. He was quite a salesman of industrial laundry machines. He turned out to be a pathological liar. After we divorced and he took est, he felt guilty about the time he forged my name on a tax refund check. We met at a bar and he gave me half that money. Years later, I got a Christmas card from Carl that said:

Joy to All -

After three vascular aorta surgeries, one bypass, three heart attacks and testicular cancer, still alive! Am single, retired and golfing two days a week. God bless your life your beautiful daughters and you and Arthur.

Merry Christmas,

Carl

After Carl, I was sure I would never marry again, but secretly I never gave up hope that one day the right man would come along. It's amazing after all these years and all those husbands, I finally got it right.

Arthur and I went to high school together back in Chicago. After one of his sons shot himself, Arthur came to Scottsdale for a rest. He looked me up in the phone book and brought me two Lalique swans. He said they reminded him of me.

The day we got married he wore a dark gray silk suit. He looked a little like a sexy hoodlum. Slicked-down hair, you know, old Chicago style. Just like Daddy.

The latest lie from Linda is that she thinks I was molested by Daddy. Honestly! She's angry with me for not protecting her when she was a child but says she understands that the same thing happened to me. Daddy? Molesting his own daughter? Ridiculous.

Ever since she started this crap, I've had to take sleeping pills and my Body Shaper del Lago business has gone straight to hell. I had a perfect location right on Scottsdale Road in a new shopping center where the Gainey Arabian horse ranch used to be.

I don't understand why this is happening. Never having been a mother herself, there's no way she could possibly understand how devastating this is. It's beyond shattering to think that a daughter of mine has all these problems.

All I ever wanted was a little girl with a rosebud mouth who would grow up to be tan and beautiful. She's my firstborn, my most important soul mate. When she was little, we modeled together in matching dresses and shorts outfits. We'd hold hands down the runway at the Westward Ho Hotel. She was so cute with her hand on her hip, her right foot pointed out in front of her, holding the skirt of her dress like an open fan. She was tall for her age. People thought she was older than she really was. I used to teach her how to say big words like homogenized.

I can't believe she doesn't remember the marvelous times of her childhood. She obviously thinks I did nothing right. I never spanked her with my hand. Just like Dr. Spock said. I always used a pancake turner.

I told her not to contact me again. "Good luck with your therapy," I said. "I sincerely hope it'll make you a happier person."

I don't feel sorry for myself. Like I told the girls, hold your head up slightly, a double chin won't show as much. If you start to cry, look up. The tears will stop and your mascara won't run.

# "Brilliantly observed and poignantly funny…"

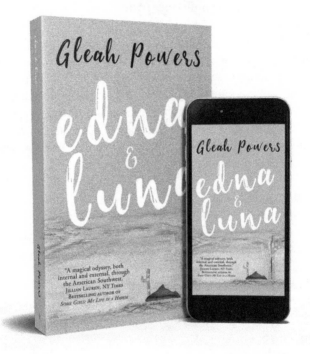

"Powers creates a world you want to stay in, characters you wish you were meeting in your own supermarket, characters you wish were knocking at your door."

CAROL POTTER, AUTHOR OF *SOME SLOW BEES*

"*Edna and Luna*, in the end, is an oasis for the human soul."

JOHN M. GIST
FOUNDING EDITOR, *RED SAVINA REVIEW*

# Acknowledgements

At Vine Leaves Press: Jessica Bell, Amie McCracken, Peter Snell, and Melissa Slayton. Lisbeth Davidow and Linda Davis for the many years of smart, generous readership in our writing group in Santa Monica. Dante Cuccinello, Sue Hogan, Louretta Walker, and Mary Shuler for their endless encouragement. Daaim Daanish for his "Projector" camaraderie and website wizardry. To my mother Gail Frew and my sister Kingsley Ann Smith, Gaines, Lang, Johnson for being. And F. X. Feeney who had a hand at every level in this book including living it. He said at CalArts over forty years ago, "You should write that down."

The following stories originally appeared, in some cases in slightly different versions, in the following publications:

"Lucky Streak," in *Souvenir Lit Journal*
"Abortos" in *Red Savina Review*
"The Three Times I Saw My Father" in *Longridge Review*
"Art Lessons" in *Prime Number Magazine*
"Pink Flamingos" in *Red Savina Review,* and as "Afros" in *Lumina*
"A Small, New Life" in *Prime Mincer Literary Journal*

*Vine Leaves Press*

Enjoyed this book?
Go to *vineleavespress.com* to find more.